DIARY OF A COLONIAL WIFE
An African Experience

DIARY OF A COLONIAL WIFE

An African Experience

Joan Sharwood-Smith

Radcliffe Press

Published in 1992 by the Radcliffe Press
110 Gloucester Avenue
London NW1 8JA

An imprint of I.B. Tauris & Co Ltd

In the United States of America
and Canada distributed by
St Martin's Press
175 Fifth Avenue
New York
NY 10010

A CIP record for this book is available from the British Library

Library of Congress Catalog card number is available
A full CIP record is available from the Library of Congress

ISBN 1-870915-12-7

Typeset by Scribe Design, Gillingham, Kent
Printed and bound in Great Britain by
Bookcraft Ltd, Midsomer Norton, Avon.

CONTENTS

PREFACE

The 'Mem Sahib' used generally to be given a bad character in literature. From the more lurid fiction you might almost suppose that the hand that rocked the cradle lost the Empire. The love affair in the languorous setting, the gin bottle, the insults to the 'native' have provided good copy for the novelist and entertainment for the reader but reality was different. It was less highly coloured, far more varied and often a great deal more interesting. At least the author found it so in Northern Nigeria. This book tells the story of a colonial service wife extending nearly twenty years, from the beginning of the Second World War to the eve of Nigerian independence. It was a hard time but also a fortunate one since the war and then headlong progress towards independence kept at bay that bugbear of the colonial wife – boredom. This only existed when the wife was unable to contribute much towards her husband's work and merely had to provide for him a passive, domestic background devoid of any real family life.

No sooner had the author arrived in 1939 than she had to learn her husband's strange life of lonely stations, horse treks, encounters with snakes in bat-ridden rest houses, to get to know the language and the people. It was just as well that she did, for with the fall of France in 1940, Nigeria became a frontier province, her husband an army officer in charge of transfrontier intelligence, herself his adjutant and cypher clerk and hostess to escaping Free French officers and to General de Gaulle himself.

Then came the family and the traditional dilemma of the colonial wife, torn between husband and children. For them it was not so bad, for, thanks to progess in medicine, they were the first generation to have their children with them, at least for part of the time. They were the first generation and the last, for as they grew up there began Nigeria's race towards self-rule. This accounts for the feel of the latter part of the book, in which family and public life are inextricably interwoven. This was natural in a society in which the family has always been the dominant institution, as it still is. In this male-dominated society, Islamic, patriarchal and colonial, the lady in the big house played a role which even the exacting feminists of a later generation must find vital and engrossing.

Later, Sir Bryan Sharwood-Smith, as Governor of Northern Nigeria, was responsible for the last great Durbar of Empire, when he had the honour of the visit of the Queen and Prince Philip; he also presided over the preparation of the North for independence. British and Northern Nigerians worked enthusiastically side by side on the transition from feudalism to democracy while retaining the more valuable traditions of the country. The politicians, new to power, were sometimes in conflict with one another or with their chiefs but there was always co-operation, partnership and friendship. Many became friends of the family, the first Prime Minister of Nigeria, for example, Sir Abubakar Tafewa Balewa and the Northern Premier, the Sardauna of Sokoto, later Sir Ahmadu Bello. Both were subsequently assassinated, the latter with his chief wife, in the *coup d'état* which started the terrible cycle of events, culminating in the tragic civil war. In those years the author and her husband had to mourn many friends and what seemed like the destruction of the country and people that had been their life.

The title of Sir Bryan's impressive memoir of his Nigerian career is *But Always as Friends*; and it well describes his widow's experience. During her husband's long last illness they were visited in their Sussex home by many old Nigerian friends and received many tokens of abiding affection from the people among whom they had lived and worked for so long. This ample affection, kindness and personal interest, so typical of the Nigerian temperament, extends to the whole family, as Joan and the children found at the time of Bryan's death and afterwards. This is not a political book, but the network of personal relations described in it, replicated many times in Nigeria and other ex-colonies, was the safety net underlying the hazardous transition from Empire to Commonwealth. It has stood the test of time and of the ups and downs of Nigerian domestic politics and of Anglo-Nigerian relations.

It is strange to pass into history during one's lifetime. Yet this is what has happened to a whole generation of colonial civil servants and their wives. This story is, then a period piece, a record of a way of life that will never be repeated. The end of

Empire is at last falling into perspective. After painfully averting our eyes, there is a new quickening of interest. This is a view from the distaff side of the making of history. It tells what it was like during a crucial time to be what, in Hausa, they call '*Uwargida*', the mother of the house.

Maurice Latey
May 1988

MAURICE LATEY OBE

Maurice Latey was a writer and broadcaster on international affairs, author of *Tyranny; a study in the Abuse of Power* (Macmillan 1969, Pelican paperbacks 1972). As editor of BBC news to Germany during the war, and of BBC broadcasts to the USSR and Eastern Europe subsequently, he has devoted special study to the rise and fall of empires. As Editor of talks and Features and Chief Commentator of the BBC World Service, he was struck by the contrast between the treatment in the media of the transition from Empire to Commenwealth and the accounts given by those actually engaged in this difficult operation.

Maurice Latey wrote in a recent contribution to 'The World Today' (Royal Institute of International Affairs): 'It is surely time that just as the USA has emerged from its post-Vietnam syndrome, the Bristish media should cast off their post-Suez, post-imperial hangover'. He regards Sir Bryan Sharwood-Smith's '*But Always as Friends*' and Lady Sharwood-Smith's companion work as valuable contributions to this re-assesment.

PART ONE

1
VOYAGE TO ADVENTURE

My story begins in 1939, just after the beginning of the Second World War. I was newly married and in my early twenties. Bryan, my husband, sixteen years my senior, was in the Nigerian Civil Service. At the time of our wedding, he was on leave in England. Just a few days after, he was called up to serve in the Nigeria Regiment in which he had been a reserve officer for many years, and it was only a week later that he left by troopship for Nigeria. When he said 'Goodbye' on the boat train platform of Waterloo Station, we had no idea when or where we should meet again. However, on arrival at Lagos he was given instructions to return to his civilian post in the administration. He was needed far more there than in the army. This was naturally a great disappointment for him, but there was a brighter side, for it meant that I could join him.

Indeed, in his next letter, Bryan told me that he had already booked my sea passage and for only three weeks ahead, so there was no time to lose. Most important, he went on in his letter, I must get myself inoculated against yellow fever, buy myself a double terai and take a trial dose of quinine. This was then the only antidote to malaria. Ex-patriats did not have any natural immunity against this disease, but a small daily dose of quinine gave them some protection. Bryan said that I should start by taking a '3 gr,' dose of quinine. Or was it a '3 go' dose? The writing was not clear. I asked my chemist and was told that quinine was only made in 5-grain tablets, wrongly, as I soon found out. For after taking the full 15 grains my teeth started chattering and bells rang madly in my ears and I could not stop shivering. I was in Leamington, staying with my parents at the time. My father consulted his medical book of reference and discovered that there was a disease called 'Blackwater fever' brought on by excessive doses of quinine. It was often fatal, especially to those living in the tropics. I went to bed clutching my hot water bottle, fearing the

3

worst. The next morning I was relieved to find that, though a little shaky, I was otherwise none the worse and well enough to plan a visit to London. Having had my yellow fever jab at the hospital for tropical diseases, I set out to buy myself a double terai. I hadn't the faintest idea what it could be. I only knew that I had to buy it at Fortnum and Masons. On entering the store I had to pass through the luxury foodstuffs department to the back of the shop from which a tiny box-like lift took me to the Equipment Department, on the 4th floor. There they had literally everything that anyone could want in the remotest outpost of the Empire. There were tropical garments, camp chairs and tables, canvas baths, Tilley lamps, water filters, saddlery and mosquito nets. The double terai turned out to be two felt hats, one to be worn on top of the other as a protection against the tropical sun. It was a pity that I chose a white one, for it showed every mark of Nigerian red dust and in those days there were no dry cleaners.

The wife of one of Bryan's friends had been asked to send me a list of the clothes I should need. In her reply, she said 'Be sure to buy twelve cotton dresses, six semi-evening dresses and a dozen of every form of underwear. Don't forget,' she ended, 'to bring mosquito boots.' Once more I repaired to Fortnum and Mason's Equipment Department where I selected an elegant pair, again unfortunately white ones. They had long pointed toes and waisted heels and extended to the tops of my thighs. As for the rest of the list, I divided the numbers by half since I did not want to leave England heavily in the red. This, however, was precisely what most people going to Nigeria did, repaying their debt by instalments during their 'tour' in the country.

Despite these reductions, 1 November 1939 found me standing nervously on the boat train platform of Euston with no less than seven uniform cases and six pieces of hand-baggage. I had never before travelled with so much luggage but I later discovered another wife travelling with fifty packing cases and she seemed quite unconcerned. Secrecy about ships was of the greatest importance and I had been warned to speak to no one of my destination and to label my luggage with my name and a code number. 'Going to West Africa, Miss?' a porter asked me, as the train came into the platform. Not knowing how to answer this without committing an offence against the Official Secrets Act, I just nodded. 'Then this way.' He led me to a compartment, on the window of which was a slip bearing my name. I said 'Goodbye' to my parents, the whistle blew and out steamed the train. Except for a middle-aged man who looked unconversational, the compartment was empty and I hoped for a quiet journey. However, before long I heard female voices in the corridor and, through the steamy glass, I distinctly heard them mention my name. Yet, I was quite sure I had never seen them before. It was very puzzling. They moved on and presently two more came and studied my name slip with the same curiosity. Why should they be so interested in me, a complete stranger? At this stage, I did not realise what a 'small' world Nigeria was for the white people working there, despite the great distances which separated one 'station' from another. Bryan had already served in the country for eighteen years so was naturally well-known. His many friends and acquaintances were most intrigued to hear that he had just re-married since, owing to the outbreak of the war, the grapevine had failed to operate. His first marriage had ended three years before we first met.

We sailed from Liverpool under leaden skies and with slight fog. Already, there were plenty of German U boats in the Atlantic and a pocket battleship, the *Deutschland*, as well, so life-boat drill was a serious matter and we were ordered to take our life-jackets with us everywhere. The ship was systematically blacked out at night and there was no changing for dinner nor dancing. It was not until we were actually on board that we even discovered the name of our ship, which was the *Abosso*. She was the queen of the Elder Dempster's fleet of West African Mail ships and fast enough to travel unescorted. Fortunately, it was a peaceful voyage, apart from some distant gunfire heard one night as we lay motionless off the coast of Wales and, later in the journey, a whale was mistaken for a German U boat which caused us violently to zig-zag until it was identified.

On the second evening I was approached by a gaunt, weedy man. 'You are Mrs Sharwood-Smith, I believe,' he began. 'I know your husband.'

He was not the first to have said these words. However, I tried to look interested. After a few minutes' conversation, he asked, 'Do you know anything about the insect-born diseases of West Africa?'

'Well, not much,' I rashly admitted. I was then treated to a long lecture on malaria, dysentery and black water fever which I endured without much flinching, but when he came to personal experiences of bilharzia, sparing no details, I began to feel a little dizzy. To make matters worse, the *Abosso* was executing the corkscrew roll, typical of all West African mail ships in these days owing to their shallow draught. Noticing my pallor, another passenger found me a seat into which I sank gratefully. The next two days, I was one of the many who did not appear. By the fourth day, feeling a little better, I dressed shakily and made my way up on deck. There, in deck chairs, firmly wrapped in rugs, I found a row of fellow sufferers. The weather improved steadily and by one o'clock we were able to enjoy a picnic of chicken sandwiches and champagne, thoughtfully ordered by one of the men. By the next morning most of us were well enough to take breakfast in the dining saloon. I was sharing a table with an army wife and a nursing sister. Soon after we had taken our seats, three large men with florrid faces pushed past our table, talking loudly and smelling unmistakably of alcohol.

'Old Coasters!' whispered the army wife.

'Do they always drink before breakfast?' I asked.

'Oh yes, brandy and ginger, it cures hangovers,' she replied. Obviously it also improved the appetite, for presently a steward arrived at their table with a gargantuan tray-load of omelettes, kidneys and bacon. The old coasters attacked their food with relish and it was not until they had finished that they paused to look around them. They appeared to be noticing that most of the places which had been empty the day before were now filled. Then we heard one of them say gruffly, 'Awful, all these women coming out, spoiling the country!'

After breakfast, deck games began. I found that I had been fortunate enough to have drawn a Greek ex-Davis Cup player as my partner for the deck quoits. He gave me painstaking lessons with the result that we won the tournament.

A few days later, we officially entered the tropics. The three old coasters now appeared at breakfast in khaki knee-length shorts, looking like musical comedy boy scouts. Everyone wore terais or Bombay bowlers on the open deck between nine o'clock in the morning and five in the afternoon. I was reproved by an older woman for appearing hatless just after breakfast.

As the sun grew warmer, everyone seemed more relaxed. Rounds of drinks before lunch and dinner were longer and more leisurely and between two and five in the afternoon there was silence while passengers snoozed in deck chairs or retired to the cool of their cabins for a siesta. After tea, the setting sun shone brassily over a calm and oily sea. Very quickly darkness fell. After dinner, I used to meet some friends on the after hatch. In the darkness of the blacked-out ship, we amused ourselves by playing gramophone records or listening to one of the party playing his guitar and singing ballads. He had a wide repertoire, ranging from the mildly bawdy to the sentimental. I often used to wonder how far away we were visible, for sparks from the funnel frequently seemed to betray us and the foam churned up by our bows was brilliant with phosphorescence. In the dark blue vault of the night sky the stars shone with added intensity. The whole atmosphere had changed. Further north it had been cold and remote, now it was warm and yielding.

Being the only Administrative bride on board, I was an easy target for the customary teasing.

'Do you realise the importance of the Middle belt and the Tsetse belt?' someone solemnly asked me.

'No!' I exclaimed, 'Can I buy them in Lagos?'

There were roars of laughter while it was explained that these were geographical names for certain parts of Nigeria. Then they tried the usual tall stories about flying scorpions. When they went on to insist that all brides, on arrival at Lagos, were invited to spend the day at Government House, I just laughed, though they assured me that this was so. Indeed, I sincerely hoped that they were joking!

We were due to reach Lagos early in the morning and to leave for the North by the up-country express at ten o'clock the same night. I pictured myself spending the intervening hours strolling alone along the Marina, stopping occasionally at a café for a cool drink where I should sit on a whicker chair, watching the passing crowds against a background of stately palms and lapping waters. I retired to my cabin and finished packing. Through my porthole, the stately palms were already coming into view. So too were a number of imposing buildings, not at all of the type I had imagined. As I left the cabin, stewards came in and removed every piece of baggage. Meanwhile, the *Abosso* slid gracefully across the lagoon and came to rest at Apapa Wharf. A few minutes later, several well-dressed officials made their way up the gangway. To my horror, I noticed that one of these was being directed to me. It was the Governor's ADC. His Excellency had, in fact, invited me to spend the day at Government House. Before I knew where I was, I was whisked into a luxurious limousine, driven by an African chauffeur, wondering desperately what the 'drill' was. Beside me, dark and svelte, sat another district officer's wife, who knew the ropes.

'It is perfectly simple,' she assured me, 'just be natural!'

This was not exactly helpful and much easier for her than for me, for she had brought a valise containing two changes of clothes; sports clothes for the afternoon and an evening dress for dinner. Noone had told me of this. Our hostess, Lady Bourdillon, was very kind, and did her best to put me at ease. During dinner, I even ventured to ask HE where the machine was that worked the punkahs, four parallel canvas frills which fluttered majestically to and fro over the dinner table, fanning the guests. He told me they were operated by two 'boys' who spent the whole of every meal time pulling concealed ropes. I was quite shocked that human beings should be made to perform so mechanical a task. Had I known more about Africa, I should have realised that, far from feeling resentful, these servants were quite likely to be sitting happily propped against a wall, the rhythm of their task having lulled them into a state of blissful trance.

HE then asked me if I knew what languages were spoken in Northern Nigeria and I replied brightly 'Hausa'. I had already learnt several basic expressions on the voyage.

'Hausa,' said His Excellency, 'is only one of many different languages spoken in the North.'

I was not sorry when the time came to drive to the station. A sleeper had been prepared for me and soon I was asleep. About an hour later, I awoke to find that the train had stopped at a wayside station. Hearing sing-song voices, I peeped out of my window and could just see, in the darkness, the shapes of some Yoruba women traders. They had large baskets balanced on their heads containing loaves of bread which they were hawking to African passengers. The station building was a dim concrete block with a corrugated iron roof. Beside it, a footpath led down a grassy slope to a village, a group of silent cottages, partly hidden by high grass. Beyond the village, silhouetted against the moon, were towering trees, typical of the tropical rain belt. The still, warm air rang with the noise of crickets. My imagination leapt into the forest, where I pictured monkeys swinging from tree to tree, snakes and other reptiles crawling amongst the undergrowth and birds of brilliant hue, resting among the leaves. Happily, I went to sleep again.

When I awoke the next morning, the high forest had disappeared. Instead, we were making our way very slowly uphill through stunted and monotonous woodland. I strained my eyes, searching between the tree trunks for some sign of game, but no living thing seemed to stir in this leafy wilderness. Despite appearances, it was not uninhabited, for presently we pulled up at another small station. This time, the hawkers were selling oranges and bananas. One or two European passengers joined in the bargaining and impressed me with the volubility of their Hausa.

Towards midday, I joined several of my new friends from the *Abosso* who were also northward-bound. 'When we cross Jebba Bridge,' they told me, 'there is a wonderful view.' Apart from being beautiful, Jebba was exceedingly hot and as we reached it at two in the afternoon, I was far too uncomfortable to appreciate the scenerey. Relief came, but not until sunset and by this time we were nearing Zungeru where Bryan was awaiting me. The little station was in almost complete darkness. As Bryan came along the platform in my direction, he was just a familiar shape for I could not see his face. Once we were together, it began to seem faintly possible that this strange country might one day seem like home.

Bryan's title was 'SDO Kontagora'. Zungeru was in the 'parish' and eighty miles from Kontagora, the divisional headquarters. As it was too late to drive to Kontagora that night, it had been arranged that we should stay at Zungeru rest-house. This was a round, mud house, with a conical thatched roof and was perched at the top of a rocky slope which led down to the Kaduna River. As we sat under the stars, eating a three-course dinner on canvas chairs at a camp table, we could hear water roaring over the rapids of the nearby Kaduna river. Bryan told me that he had shot a crocodile there that very morning. We bathed in a canvas bath inside the building but slept outside in a small fenced enclosure. Although the camp beds were not uncomfortable, I was too excited for sleep. Moreover, the moon was so bright that I could feel its glow through my closed eyelids. Strange animals and birds croaked and squawked all through the night.

The next morning, after an early breakfast, we left by road for Kontagora. It seemed a long and monotonous eighty miles. As we drove into the station, men and women curtseyed at the roadside in greeting. Some of them raised a clenched fist.

'Why are they doing that and what are they saying?' I wanted to know.

Poor Bryan. This was just the beginning of my questions.

'The clenched fist symbolises the shaking of a spear, which was the old-time salute. They are saying '*Ranka shi dade*!' which means "May your life be long!"'

Just then, we came to a crossroads where a policeman in a red fez, butcher-blue shorts and a tunic, tightly belted at the waist by a crimson cummerbund was on point duty. He saluted smartly, then waved us across, halting an imaginary column of traffic with the other hand. As our car turned into the district officer's compound and crunched to a standstill on the gravel, another policeman, poised at the flag staff, raised the Union Jack.

2 FIRST IMPRESSIONS

The District Officer's bungalow was a long, thatched building with verandahs running along the whole length of the front and back. Inside, I was surprised to find comfortable easy chairs, cushions and carpets, for deck chairs and rush mats were all that I had expected. Attached to the walls were Bryan's hunting trophies; the skulls of horned animals, mounted on wooden shields. The cranium of a boar with fearsome tusks especially caught my eye.

'I'll tell you the story of each one some time,' Bryan said. 'Now come and see the rest of the house.'

He led me through double doors into a dark, narrow room. In the middle, pushed close together, were two monstrous, black iron bedsteads of a type supplied in those days to all government quarters by the Public Works Department. Their mattresses were waist high and, from the four corners, iron posts, surmounted by brass knobs, practically reached the ceiling. These knobs were linked above by rails from which hung, limp and drab, a regulation double mosquito net. I sighed. 'Don't worry,' Bryan reassured me, 'from now until the rains we shall be able to sleep outside.' It was then the end of November, the beginning of the dry season. With any luck, not a drop of rain would fall until the following March.

'When you have seen the house, you'd better meet the staff.'

Usuman, the head steward, was presented to me first. He was followed by Tanko, the second steward and then came Musa, the 'small boy'.

'He cleans boots and runs errands,' Bryan explained. "Usuman" is the same as "Ottoman", and "Musa" is "Moses".'

Finally, along came two elderly men with wispy beards and what looked like tattered nightshirts. They were Ibrahim and Isa, the gardeners.

"Ibrahim" equals "Abraham" and "Isa" is "Jesus",' he added.

'But I thought you said they were all Muslims,' I protested.

'Why do most of them have names from the Bible?'

11

'Well, you see, the Koran and the Bible have much in common,' was the reply. 'Oh no, don't shake hands with them, that would shock them deeply. You only shake hands with the chiefs. Just smile and say "*Sanu*".'

So I said my '*Sanu*' to these mainly biblical characters. The three house 'boys' with their bland, black faces, white skull caps and shapeless white gowns looked exactly alike to me and it was several days before I was able to distinguish between them with any certainty.

'Usuman is devoted to me and very sensitive. If you say anything to upset him, he may fly off the handle like an opera singer,' Bryan warned me.

Obviously the cobwebs I had just noticed would have to stay where they were until we were better acquainted, unless I found a broom and removed them myself, but that, I felt, would be undignified.

The cook, who had been to the market, returned just then on his bicycle. He was brought to meet me. Being a Southerner and mission-trained, he wore European clothes; a pair of khaki shorts and a striped shirt, open at the neck and rather dirty. 'He is quite new and doesn't understand a word of any known language except a little pidgin English', I was told. 'But don't worry about him for the present. I will give him his orders for the first week.'

As Cook's name was quite unpronounceable, I soon dropped into the habit of calling him 'Kuku', the Hausa version of the English word 'Cook'.

At my first interview with Kuku, I tried to speak very slowly and distinctly so as to help him to understand. The head butcher from the town was with him, a hatchet-faced old man in a dark blue turban and faded gown. He had called for orders. 'Tell him I should like some veal cutlets, about a pound and a half,' I said. They gazed at me blankly. I amplified, 'Young cow, baby cow,' making gestures to indicate the size of the animal and the portion required. It was no good. Neither of them had understood.

'Well, what kind of meat has he?' I asked.

In reply they both said 'Oomp.' Mentally, I went through all the joints enumerated in Mrs Beeton's illustrations of the sheep and ox. None seemed to approach this word. In the end, I said, 'Well, we will try it.' It was the hump of an ox and, strangely enough, did taste something like veal, though the texture was tougher.

A hundred or so yards from the DO's house was another similar bungalow, supposed to be occupied by an assistant district officer but it was empty. There were very few young administrative officers, as most of them had been called up for war service with the Nigeria Regiment. The only other European at Kontagora was the agricultural officer, who lived four miles the other side of the town and was practically always on tour. Occasionally, visitors came through the station from Minna, the provincial headquarters or from Bida where our doctor lived. Both were over a hundred miles away. Yet, it so happened that during my first few weeks in Kontagora, we scarcely saw another white face.

Bryan used to go to his office, a flat-roofed, mud building which looked more like a barn, at half-past seven every morning. He returned for breakfast regularly at half-past nine and by ten o'clock he was away again until three in the afternoon, when he returned for lunch. 'No wife with any brains is ever bored in Nigeria. There is so much in the country of interest,' I remember being told on board the *Abosso* by those who should know. Nevertheless, after an hour of sitting reading or knitting, the time was still only eleven, and there seemed to be nothing else to do until lunch time, three solid hours away. Perhaps I could be taking an interest in the house and indeed I had made some tactful suggestions to Usuman about ways in which 'we' might improve it, but he seemed quite unable to understand my English. Tanko and Musa spoke nothing but Hausa.

'So much in the country of interest,' I repeated to myself one morning when the silence of the DO's house had become more than I could bear. 'Well, why not go out and find it?' I put on my terai and sunglasses and set forth in the blazing sun. Following a footpath which led across the park-like clearing surrounding the DO's house, I soon found myself in the bush. It so happened that Bryan returned from his office early that day and was horrified when he found me not there.

'Where is missus?'

Usuman did not know. He had been asleep under a mango tree just outside the boy's quarters. At last a policeman was found who said he had seen me walking down the path leading to the bush. He had probably thought me quite mad, like all white women. So I was discovered, not far away, sitting on an anthill and watching some lizards.

'Really,' Bryan protested, 'You mustn't go wandering about the bush by yourself like that. There are such things as dangerous animals and dangerous people too, religious fanatics for instance.'

He then told me how he himself had been attacked by two Muslim fanatics only a few years before.

There had been several outbreaks of religious violence about this time and one district officer had been seriously wounded. 'Even now,' Bryan concluded, 'There are dangerous men amongst the mentally unhinged and you find them sometimes, wandering by themselves in the bush.'

That dangerous animals, and particularly reptiles, existed I was soon to discover for myself. Bryan told the policeman normally on duty guarding the house, to follow me if I went out by myself again. I did, of course, repeatedly, and found that trying to elude 'my' policeman was an excellent cure for boredom.

All the same, it was obvious that some kind of useful occupation was required. So I was made an honorary member of the office staff, with the task of tidying the library and copying the Emir's family tree which hung behind the office door in a state of faded dilapidation. This fascinating document took the Emir's family back to his great grandfather, Usuman dan Fodio, the religious reformer who had founded the Fulani Empire. The Emir's father, just before the British occupation, had been a mighty slave raider and very prolific. Fifty sons were recorded on the tree, though no mention was made of the daughters. Some of the names were completely illegible, but fortunately, the officer messenger could speak a little English and by questioning the Emir's confidential messenger, he managed to supply the missing names. This Emir's representative called on the district officer as a courtesy each morning. He bore the charming title of 'Mai Ji Dadi', 'The one to feel happy', the implication being that his job was to smooth relations between the Emir and the British administration.

Of course, I wanted to learn Hausa. 'It's no use just studying a grammar. Try conversation first, then reading,' I was told. So a mallam (teacher) was sent to give me lessons every aternoon. He was a young sanitary inspector who spoke English with a cultured voice and scarcely a trace of a foreign accent. He said 'Good afternoon' then sat down. Then there was an embarrassed silence, until I realised that I should have to take the initiative.

"What is the Hausa for 'table'? I began, to which he replied, "'Tebur'". He told me how to spell it and I wrote it down.

"What is the Hausa for 'pencil'?" I asked next, and he replied, "'Pensur'".

"And for 'bread'," I continued, doggedly, and he answered "'Burodi'".

After a minute or two he said, "These are all English words." "Yes of course," I thought, "English words for English things." Just as I was feeling completely at a loss to know what to suggest next, he felt in the pocket of his voluminous gown and pulled out a child's first Hausa reader. It would have been just the thing, except that the simple words it contained, split into phonetic syllables, were of objects familiar enough to Hausa children, but largely foreign to me, such as 'calabash', 'guinea corn' and 'maize'. Obviously, I should never make progress with the language until I knew more of the Hausa way of life.

Fortunately, this did not take long. Every evening, as soon as it was cool enough, Bryan and I used to go for walks in the bush with a gun in search of bush fowl or wild guinea fowl and we usually came back through the sun-baked streets of Kontagora town, about two miles from the government station. The houses consisted of groups of thatched mud huts surrounded by plaited grass or corn stalk fences or high mud walls. Each hut was the equivalent of a room. There was one large one for the master of the house and smaller ones for each of his wives and these might number up to four. Another hut was the kitchen, distinguished from the others by the smoke which seeped through the thatch for these was no chimney. Then there were one or two very small huts on stilts, used as bins for storing guinea corn, millet or maize, the staple foods. The calabashes, which were used instead of cups and basins, were made from the hard shells of gourds which grew like marrows along the ground. Some climbed up the walls of the huts and produced their fruit on the roof-tops. Donkeys, sheep, goats and poultry wandered in and out of the houses and across the streets.

When we returned from our evening's exercise, Usuman and Tanko were called to move easy chairs and carpets from the house into the garden, for we always sat outside after dark. After half and hour's relaxation with a cool drink, we used to shout in the ringing tones which one acquired after a little practice, "Boooooy!" From the distance, no matter which of us had called, in the back of the compound came a faint answering shout of "Sir!" Nothing happened for two or three minutes, then finally a boy appeared and was asked to bring bath water. This had been heated in petrol cans over log fires somewhere at the back of the compound and was usually carried into the bathroom by the perspiring Musa, who staggered as he ran with his scalding burden. Petrol or kerosene (paraffin) cans were always used in place of buckets with their lids cut away and a handle of wood nailed across the top. After bathing, we changed into clean clothes and then reclined in our easy chairs for the rest of the evening with only the stars for illumination and a spluttering Tilley lamp which was placed on a stand some distance away for it attracted insets. Moths, praying mantises, sausage flies and winged beetles whirred round the lamp in ever narrowing spirals. Usuman sometimes placed a large basin of water under the lamp and in no time it was filled with wriggling bodies. A long gin and lime was my idea of a refreshing drink after a hot day but I was told that gin would make me depressed and that I must learn to drink whisky. So I did, though at first with a wry face. It was a lesson Bryan might have regretted later, when the whisky ration was reduced to only one bottle a month per household.

When the time came for our evening meal, Usuman was summoned once more, this time with the cry of "*Kawo abinci*" ("Bring food"). He disappeared and returned presently with Tanko, carrying the table, cutlery etc., for we dined outside. Just before turning into our beds, which were concealed behind the rush fence, as at Zungeru, we often saw antelope, feeding in the valley by moonlight. Occasionally, during the night we were awakened by the howl of a hyena or cough of a leopard and once or twice we heard a lion roaring.

Our little brown terrier, Toby, used to sleep inside our fence, chained to one of the posts. We dared not loose him for fear of his wandering into the bush during the night and being seized by some wild animal. Bryan always slept at night with his shot gun beside him. One night, Toby woke me out of a deep sleep by violent barking. 'Stop it, Toby!' I yelled out sleepily. Then, as the barking continued more desperately than ever, I thought perhaps I had better investigate. So I switched on my torch and was horrified to see an enormous cobra just beside my bed, its hood inflated, obviously just about to strike at poor Toby. I shook Bryan, who awoke to the situation with remarkable speed. Seizing his shot gun, he slipped in the two cartridges which he kept under his pillow, and shot the head off the snake. Off too went the terrified Toby, snapping his chain, straight through the fence and away into the bush. It was a long time before we managed to retrieve and calm him so that we could all resume our night's sleep.

One day, Bryan said, 'I have to inspect the prison today. Would you like to come with me? I am afraid you will not be allowed to go inside.' Of course I said 'Yes.' Anything for a change. We took

the road to the town and Bryan pulled up in the shade of a locust bean
tree, opposite the prison. He was met by the chief warder, a tall man
dressed in a red and white striped tunic and a red turban. Together
they disappeared behind the prison's high mud wall and the iron
gates clanged behind them. I remained inside the car, with 'my'
policeman, watching passers by. Hordes of naked children, pot-
bellied and full of mischief, collected round the car, just as fascinated
by me as I was by them. The policeman got out and sternly shooed
them away, but they came back as soon as they dared. Two men
in long robes and turbans then came along and as they passed,
saluted me with *'Sanu, uwargida!'* meaning 'Greetings, mother-of-
the-house!' a courtesy title for the head wife of a household. Soon
came a train of Fulani women on their way to market from their encampment a few miles away in the bush. The Fulani are cattle-owning
nomads, living in cornstalk wigwams and moving periodically from
one pasture to another. Every day their women-folk walked to the
nearest market to sell their dairy produce. These women were light
copper coloured, slim and graceful, and they wore silver earrings
and beaded bangles. Each one had a calabash on her head containing
sour milk or butter. Two of them had babies tied to their backs, with
strong homespun cloth so that only the baby's woolly head appeared.
One of the mothers stooped to pick something from the ground.
As she bent her knees, her calabash remained beautifully poised
and the baby undisturbed. Presently, the other baby began to cry
and was pulled round, on to his mother's hip, so as to suck from
her breast. All the while, the procession moved onward with an
easy grace worthy of any school of deportment.

The Emir, in his Chevrolet saloon, followed by a lorry-load of
councillors and personal servants, made a courtesy call at the
district officer's house regularly once a week. On these occasions,
I was banished from our one living room. I usually sat on one of
the iron bedsteads reading a book, distracted by the fluctuation of
male voices in the next room and the aroma of oriental perfumes.
When the business of the day was done, Bryan used to call me to
shake hands with the Emir and exchange more distant greetings
with the retainers. My efforts to speak Hausa caused the Emir to
chuckle with delight. I was quite captivated by the old man, with
his kind, expansive smile and amply flowing robes. Beneath the
twist of his muslin turban was the head of a fine, old ruler, full of
wit and wisdom.

Soon, I set out on my first bush trek. The first seven miles we
were to travel by light lorry. The rest of the journey lay along bridle

paths, not motorable, even by Nigerian standards. Our ponies with their grooms were sent ahead the day before. The following morning, we were called at five o'clock and dressed while it was still dark. Even as we climbed into the lorry, the stars still shone in the sky. Usuman, Tanko, Kuku and Umaru, the messenger, were already sitting in the back of the van, amongst a collection of packing cases, kettles and rolled up mats collectively known as 'the loads'. Then away we went with cries of 'Goodbye' and 'Return safely!' from Isa and Ibrahim the gardeners, the only members of the staff left behind.

The road was narrow, rough and undulating. We threaded our way over a bridge with great precision, for the slightest deviation would have tipped us over the edge into a dried up stream ten feet below. After five miles, we passed a village set against a rocky hill. Lights twinkled in every cottage doorway and the smoke of fires, which housewives had just lit to cook the morning meal, rose into the air with a pleasant, resiny smell. The sun had just risen when we reached the end of the road. There our ponies were awaiting us with a party of fifteen porters who were to carry our loads for the next six days. They were naked except for black, leather loin-cloths, and as powerful as prize-fighters.

The cook unloaded his box first from the lorry, then lit a camp fire and started cooking our breakfast. Meanwhile, the rest of the luggage was pulled out and arranged into suitable headloads, which were not supposed to exceed sixty pounds. After a lot of argument and gesticulation, the loads were raised on to the porters' heads. They set off along the bridle path in single file and were soon out of sight. That two such ordinary people, spending six days in the bush, should require such a vast collection of luggage seemed positively indecent to me. However, Bryan said firmly, 'I have done a lot of this and believe in taking my comforts with me.' Apart from suitcases, which contained clothing, there were camp-beds, chairs and tables, the canvas bath, pressure lamps, kerosene, cases of china, glass, cutlery and linen and even a gramophone, a wireless set and a box of records. One of the more important loads was the crate of groceries, always referred to as the 'chop box'. An especially careful porter was chosen to carry the wireless set. He adjusted the ring of grass which all carriers used to cushion their load, then raised his precious burden on to his head, Usuman rather unnecessarily, I thought, described to him, in pungent Hausa, what his fate would be should he dare to trip up.

Having finished our meal, we mounted and set off, accompanied by Umaru, the messenger, and the Emir's representative, also on horseback. Following on foot were the cook and another procession of carriers, bearing boxes of pots and pans. Usuman brought up the rear, his closest personal possessions rolled into a mat on his head and his private kettle in his hand. His hurt expression was meant to show how strongly he disapproved of bush whacking, which he felt was undignified for the head steward of so senior a DO. Meanwhile, we pushed on at a steady canter and soon overtook the first party of carriers.

My pony was a chestnut stallion, the first I had ever owned. We bought him for £10, an average price for a trek pony in Nigeria in those days. Bryan's was a stocky, Sokoto black of uncertain temper.

The bridle path led through woodland, stunted and spindly. The grass was already tinder dry. Soon bush fires would sweep over the landscape, leaving vast tracks of land black and smouldering. Then, within a few days, vivid green grass would miraculously shoot up from amongst the ashes and resplendent leaf burst forth from the charred trees. District officers tried to persuade the Fulani to burn the bush early in the season, for if left until late there was danger of the trees being totally destroyed. The Fulani lit bush fires deliberately, to provide green grass for their cattle.

As the sun grew hotter, we slowed down from a smart canter to a leisurely shamble. Then I noticed a black, rocky hill standing like a giant pimple amongst the trees.

'Only three more miles,' Bryan called out, 'the village where we are spending the night is close to that hill.'

By this time, the sun was almost overhead. Soon we were met by the village head with a party of retainers. They were mounted on gorgeously-caparisoned horses. With my plain English saddlery, I felt positively mousy. The village head's horse tossed his head and pawed the ground and the ornaments jingled. Then he and his followers turned and led the way to the Rest House. This was a large, circular mud building with a thatched roof. Inside, it was completely bare. At the back was a row of little mud huts, small replicas of the main building intended for the servants. In front, was a rickety flag pole. The messenger had cantered ahead with the Union Jack, so that the moment our feet touched the ground, up went the flag. This showed that the white visitor at the Rest House was the District Officer and if anyone had a grievance, this was their opportunity to come to tell him. An old man in a tattered gown greeted us with 'Blessings on your dismounting!' and 'May you live long!' This was the caretaker of the Rest House, picturesquely known in Hausa as the 'Sarikin bariki' or 'king of the barracks'. The caretaker's child, a waif of about seven, dressed in what looked like a night shirt, was standing behind his father. There was a calabash on his head containing eggs and onions and in his hand he clutched a couple of squawking hens, tied together by the legs.

Until the carriers arrived, there was nothing to sit on and my legs ached, so Bryan asked the caretaker to produce a couple of *turmis*. The child disappeared and presently returned with another even smaller boy. They were carrying on their heads what appeared to be giant egg cups, roughly hewn from wood. These they placed, upside down, on the floor and I was invited to sit on one while Bryan perched himself on the other.

'Are these meant for sitting on?' I asked.

'No, they are used the other way up by the women as mortars for pounding grain.'

Then I remembered many times having seen them in use in Kontagora.

Bryan did not remain seated long. In no time, he was striding off to the village on a tour of inspection, followed by the faithful Umaru. Left alone, sitting on my turmi, I thought longingly of stretching myself full length on the ground, but it was rough and dusty and there were large black ants scurrying across it. After what seemed like hours, the first carriers arrived and some camp furniture was unpacked. I sank gratefully into a deck chair.

The boys were surprisingly cheerful after their long walk. Even Usuman managed to smile a greeting. Without pausing to rest, they set to work unfolding beds and tables and laying down mats. Bottles of drinking water, beer and soda were pulled out of crates and placed in earthenware pitchers which the caretaker had already filled with water. Being porous, these made remarkably efficient coolers, especially when placed in a draught. By the time Bryan returned, the beer was cool enough to drink.

Every bush rest house, I discovered, had its family of resident bats. During the day, they hitched themselves by one leg to the rafters, emitting a loathsome, tarry smell. They woke up at night and swooped to and fro across the interior of the rest house, uttering shrill cries. Once, sitting in four inches of muddy water in the canvas bath, trying to cleanse myself, one of the bats swooped so low over my head that it almost touched my hair. I called out in a panic, but by the time Bryan arrived to my rescue, the bat had settled on the floor close to the bath. As it lay softly in the lamp light it looked gentle and mouse-like. All the same, I asked Bryan to kill it and reluctantly he did.

I met my first snake two nights later. It was a sand viper. It wriggled straight past me and away into the bush, leaving a half-eaten toad. Thereafter, Usuman was told to inspect the darker parts of the rest house regularly with a bush lamp to scare off undesirable reptiles.

3 TRANSFRONTIER INTELLIGENCE

For a Nigerian, Usuman was unusually serious and moody. Before my arrival, he had served his master with single-minded devotion, priding himself on anticipating every need. Bryan, for want of other distractions, had often chatted to Usuman during the long, lonely evenings. With my arrival, this blissful master-servant relationship was shattered. He showed me his resentment by a go-slow policy of minimum co-operation. To add to his troubles, his wife was flighty. She used to sit on the wall of the servant's quarters, ogling passers by. Once he caught her in the act and gave her a beating. The whole compound resounded to his thumps and her wails. I bore with Usuman during the whole of my first tour of Nigeria, which lasted practically two years, but by the beginning of the next one he had become so difficult that we had to ask him to leave. None of his subsequent jobs lasted and he was continually coming back to see Bryan, hoping, I imagine, to be reinstated. Then he became chronically ill. We helped him by arranging courses of treatment with the nearest medical officer and although he seemed to improve a little after a course of injections, he relapsed again later.

One of the sunnier characters, on the other hand, was Umaru Dabai. Like most government messengers, he was middle-aged and an ex-army NCO. There was nothing he liked better than to be asked to tell the story of fighting the Germans in the Cameroons War, when he was awarded the DCM. His round face was fringed with a grey curly beard. He wore the usual white gown and turban and pinned to his chest was the embroidered yellow Crown, the government messengers' badge. His task was to make himself useful in the office, to keep the DO informed about what was going on in the district and to act as a go-between in domestic arrangements with district or village heads on tour. Umaru always rose magnificently to a crisis of any kind. On his off-duty evenings, he loved to be asked to accompany us on shooting expeditions. If

22

we were after duck, Umaru would plunge straight into the muddiest stream to retrieve a bird, removing only the top layer of his voluminous garments. On one of our more strenuous treks, we passed through a series of belts of high forest infested with tsetse flies. Horses are even more susceptible than human beings to the sleeping sickness which these insects carry, so we left our ponies at home and used bicycles instead. Wherever the path led through sand or over rocks, we had to dismount. Umaru would then push my bicycle, and we would plod along together, Umaru listening patiently to my halting Hausa and gently correcting me. In some places where the flies were especially persistent, walking in single file, we tore branches off trees and waved them to and fro across the back of the person in front. Despite these precautions, we were all stung viciously several times.

After four months in Kontagora, Bryan was summoned to Minna, the provincial headquarters. Mr Harris, the Resident, was due for leave and Bryan was to replace him in an 'acting' capacity. We packed our belongings and sadly said 'Goodbye' to the Emir of Kontagora, who thoroughly disapproved of 'his' district officer being changed. Bryan drove ahead in our Wolseley with Usuman, while I followed in the light lorry with Umaru. I was driving merrily along, when an enormous grasshopper flew in, crawled down my dress and embedded its powerful hind legs into the middle of my back. Uttering a screech of pain, I hastily stopped the car, leapt behind the nearest bush, tore off my dress and removed the offender. Poor Umaru stood by, utterly bewildered. My Hausa was inadequate for any explanations. We climbed back into the driver's cab in silence and continued.

At last we reached Minna and my first impression was of a town similar to Kontagora, with typically northern houses, mud-walled and opening through narrow porches on to the street. Very soon, however, the character of the place changed. The houses became more European in type, oblong with corrugated iron roofs. Many had booths in front crammed with goods for sale. One 'tailor's' shop was draped with shirts and palm beach suits. Another sold bedsteads and car parts while a slightly larger building was dignified with the name 'Hotel'. Cheap curtains stretched across its windows and from inside came the tinny strains of an outworn gramophone. Two fat women lolled beside its bead-strung entrance. Presently we passed the 'Gospel Hall', a tall, green mission building displaying a Bible text translated into Hausa. The Africans we passed were from a variety of tribes, the majority wearing European clothes which in those days indicated Southern Nigerian origin. Minna had been built when the railway was under construction and, as Northerners in those days had little in the way of western education, the clerks and artisans which the railway needed were imported from the more sophisticated coastal regions. The native people of Minna were Gwari and still lived in rocky hills surrounding the town. They were robust animists, whose women carried huge loads of firewood, arranged into inverted cone-shaped packs and balanced on the backs of their shoulders. The men farmed and kept dogs, like grey-hounds, which they regularly brought to market. The dogs were killed and eaten, for the more convenient forms of market meat were scarce and expensive. The Gwari also brewed native beer which, together with the added (canine) protein, made them look much better nourished than the more fastidious, teetotle Muslims.

Passing out of Minna town, we crossed the railway, then came to a large mission building, screened from the road by sweet smelling frangipani trees. Here young American missionaries were taught Hausa before setting forth for the field. As they were of both sexes, there was a tendency to pair off and weddings were not infrequent. Consequently, the establishment was nick-named the 'Abode of Love'. Next door was a small thatched building with a neat garden, labelled 'Minna Club'. The golf course was opposite. Finally having passed the provincial office, an ugly concrete erection, we changed down into bottom gear and started winding our way up Minna hill. Every minute, it seemed to be growing more oppressive and I was feeling both tired and apprehensive as we turned the last hairpin bend which brought us to the top.

An old-fashioned tin-roofed bungalow, with little protection from the sun, had been allotted us as temporary accommodation until the Harrises moved out of the Residency. It felt like an oven. We unpacked our room thermometer and watched the mercury rise to 106°. Presently, Bryan left for the Kingsway Stores. After Kontagora, to be able to go shopping seemed civilised indeed. Admittedly, the only European firms were the United Africa Company, which ran the Kingsway Stores, and stocked a fair range of groceries, and the Compagnie Française de l'Afrique Occidentale, commonly called the 'French Company' in Minna, which catered chiefly for Africans and sold lengths of cloth, yellow dusters and brightly enamelled bowls.

Bryan returned triumphantly twenty minutes later with two half-bottles of 'Veuve Clicquot'. We wrapped them in wet clothes and exposed them to a draught. Soon they were cool enought for consumption. I began to feel better. Perhaps life in Minna as the Acting Resident's wife would be tolerable after all.

About ten British Colonial Service officers were stationed in Minna at that time. Apart from the Resident, there were two district officers, a police officer, an engineer, a doctor, a veterinary officer, a couple of railway engineers and a mines department officer, who was concerned with a few scattered gold mines in the province. Four had wives with them, the rest being either bachelors or with wives left in the UK. There was also a bachelor bank manager. A Roman Catholic priest and two miners lived a few miles away. The American missionaries, in their 'Abode of Love' kept strictly to themselves but the rest of the white community met at weekends and of an evening at the club where they played tennis, golf or snooker or simply relaxed for a chat and a drink at the bar.

Despite the heat and the isolation, Minna was a happy little station on the whole. The kind of drama which novelists are apt to describe was rare, though Minna was reeling from the aftermath of one such incident which had occurred a few weeks before our arrival. The Irish priest, a choleric character, had, it seemed, knocked out the bank manager after a quarrel about the Pope.

The Residency was the 'big house' and invitations to meals there were coveted. Consequently, the Resident and his wife had to be careful to ask everyone in turn, with no omissions, for in a hot place like Minna people readily took offence, or 'um', (short for 'umbrage') to use the local expression.

Minna in those days was very formal. The first party to which we were invited began at eight-fifteen. Dinner was not served until ten o'clock, which gave time for so many rounds of drinks that I completely lost count. All the men and some women drank whisky, changing to pink gin just before the meal. It was not considered proper for a wife to drink level with her husband and indeed to have done so would have spelt ruin to her fading complexion. One of the women staunchly refused all alcohol and consumed glass after glass of lemon squash. Others lingered over sherry. At last, there was a signal from our hostess and the women trooped upstairs.

We ascended the stairs in strict order, according to our husband's seniority, the Resident's wife sedately leading. The operation completed, we descended the stairs in the same order and were shown our places at the dining table. A steward came with the soup and we sat there for five minutes or more watching it cool as we waited for the men. From outside came a roar of male laughter and a cry of 'Just time for one short one!' Eventually the men joined us.

Conversation at dinner ran on to the children whom many had left behind in England. There were no white children in Nigeria in those days except at the missions. The missionaries were thought to be taking an appalling risk for the belief that Nigeria was the 'White Man's Grave' persisted. Then we discussed the iniquities of cooks and finally, at about 2 a.m. Mrs Harris rose to her feet. This was the sign that the party had come to an end.

Mr and Mrs Harris were very popular and farewell parties were held in their honour at different houses on eleven of the twelve days before their departure. After the quiet life we had lived in Kontagora, we found this succession of late nights very trying. On the last occasion, we both fell asleep in our chairs after dinner, hoping, when we awoke, that in the dim light of the oil lamps, we had not been observed.

The down train to Lagos left Minna at 2.30 a.m., but that did not deter a large crowd from gathering on the platform to wave 'Goodbye' to Mr and Mrs Harris on the night of their departure. As the train steamed out, there were cries of 'Safe journey!' and we all thought of the voyage that lay before them, crossing seas where scores of thousands of tons of British shipping were being sunk each week. No doubt, the Harrises' minds were mainly on their approaching reunion with their schoolboy son whom they had not seen for nearly two years.

Bryan was silent as we drove away from the station and I guessed that he was thinking, with mixed awe and elation, of his new responsibilities. He was in charge of a province the size of Yorkshire, with a population of half a million.

Everything that went on within its borders would now be his concern. The chiefs and people would look to him and his staff for guidance and he would have control and supervision of all government activities. To help him, he had a district officer at provisional headquarters and four others, one in charge of each of the four divisions. Although the departmental officers, that is to say the medical, veterinary, agricultural and forestry officers, the engineers and the senior superintendent of Police, took their orders in technical and professional matters from their heads of department at the capital, it was for the Resident to see that they worked together harmoniously as a team, serving the best interests of the people of the province.

After the district officer's bungalow at Kontagora, the Minna Residency seemed like a palace. It was two-storeyed and set in a spacious garden. Inside were parquet floors and a profusion of glass doors and windows. In those days, government provided such furniture as chairs, beds and tables, but no soft furnishings, linens or curtains. I found to my dismay that at least 176 yards of material were required for the curtains alone if the house was to look decently furnished. I went to the Kingsway stores and the 'French Company' in search of suitable material and came back in despair. All they had to offer were flimsy prints intended for African women's wear. Then I had an idea. I had seen some attractive homespun cloth made at Bida, which was in our province about a hundred miles away. We wrote to the district officer, Bida, who sent us samples. Having made our choice, we ordered the required number which were made to measure, with fringes at the ends. They had red, green and black stripes on natural coloured cotton and between the stripes, antelopes, lizards and birds were embroidered. No two pieces of cloth were alike, but that did not seem to matter. With the curtains up, the Residency developed a new look, odd perhaps but certainly original.

The other wives in the station went out of their way to be kind and friendly to me and never showed the slightest resentment that I, a newcomer to Nigeria and still in my early twenties, was the senior wife in Minna, a position which they had done so much more to deserve. All were well into their forties, with many years experience in the country to their credit.

It was the beginning of May and the hot season was at its peak. Each day was more sultry than the last and at sunset, along the horizon, puffy clouds formed, lit from time to time by distant lightning. One evening, these clouds, instead of disappearing after a while, as on previous days, suddenly increased alarmingly in size and advanced towards us, blotting out the blue sky and growing rapidly blacker and more menacing. Usuman, Tanko and Musa appeared from nowhere and began to rush round the Residency, pulling in curtains, shutting windows and banging doors. They were only just in time, for suddenly a roaring wind arose with ear splitting claps of thunder and vivid flashes of lightning. Every sapling in the Residency garden was bent to a right angle in the gale. Branches torn off trees and debris of all kinds was hurled along by the gale. Then came the rain, horizontal and blinding, it battered violently against the window panes. Inside the house, the temperature dropped like a stone and I found myself searching in the backmost recesses of my wardrobe for something warm to wear. An hour later, the storm subsided and all was cool and calm. From then onwards, storms brewed each evening and occasionally broke on Minna. Green grass began to grow on the lawn which for months had been dry and dusty and suddenly everyone had an urge to plant something. Usuman, Tanko and Musa each laid claim to a small allotment outside the Residency grounds and whenever they were free they removed their outer garments and, stripped to the waist, tilled the soft, red earth, making holes with their big toes and dropping in the seed. Everywhere in the farmland which surrounded Minna there was joyful activity as farmers planted guinea corn, maize and ground nuts.

Once, we were playing golf on Minna's nine hole course when we noticed the familiar black clouds piling up in the East.

'That storm's coming up quickly,' Bryan said, 'We shall have to run.'

We made for the club house with all our might, but my legs were leaden.

'It's no use, I can't keep up,' I shouted. Just then, there was a searing flash of lightning and a deafening crash of thunder, followed by more flashes which seemed to strike the ground all round us.

'It might be like this in a battle,' I thought, trying not too successfully to quell my fear.

Indeed, our thoughts were very much with the war which was reaching a critical stage in Europe, as Hitler's victorious armies swept through Holland and Belgium into France. To us in Minna, BBC bulletins were the sole source of information. There were no daily newspapers. Radio reception was poor and batteries had short lives and were scarce. If, as often happened, we were invited out to drinks and the news time came, the host would sit crouched over his radio, his hand on the controls, trying to capture the distant voices from London as it faded or was drowned by blaring music from a Congo station. 'If only,' we thought, 'he would stop fiddling with those knobs, perhaps we should be able to hear too.' Then one day, the news came through that France had fallen. Britain stood alone. An awful gloom settled on Minna. Most of us had the urge to pack up and go straight home. To remain quietly in Minna doing the ordinary things of life seemed intolerable. To add to our personal feelings of frustration, our neighbours had an unusually powerful wireless set and they liked to tune in to Lord Haw Haw, the British traitor who gave the Nazi version of the news from a German station. They believed in listening to all shades of opinion. As, in Nigeria, doors and windows are normally left wide open, every word could be heard from some considerable distance. In the end, Bryan had to ask them to turn it down.

Very soon, we heard that Italy had joined the war in support of Germany. This meant that Italy's expensive African colonies were now enemy territory. The nearest was Libya, some hundreds of miles across the desert from our northern frontier. The intervening territory was in the hands of the defeated French. Although many well-defined tracks for light vehicles crossed the Sahara, it was considered impassable to heavy traffic. Consequently, it was thought safe to send a brigade of Nigerian troops to East Africa to fight the Italians in Abyssinia. The troop trains passed through Minna, halting for an hour. This gave us time to meet army friends passing through and take them to the Residency for refreshments.

With the departure of nearly all trained troops, Nigeria was left almost defenceless. We knew that there was no immediate danger, but should the war in Africa take the same disastrous turn as in Europe, it seemed to us that Nigeria might well one day be attacked. Bryan, of his own initiative formed a Defence Force in Minna, modelled on the Local Defence Volunteers, later called the Home Guard, which were being formed all over Britain. The idea was greeted with enthusiasm, especially with those Britons and Nigerians who had served in the First World War. The 'Minna Militia' drilled at the airport three times a week and at other times it was engaged in making home-made explosives and practising rifle shooting. I also learnt to shoot and spend periodic half hours on the police range, lying on my tummy and bruising my shoulder. The news of Bryan's initiative was received coolly at Kaduna, the Northern Nigerian capital. Plans for the establishment of local defence forces all over the region were under consideration. He should have awaited instructions.

Bryan then developed an infected wisdom tooth. There was no dentist in Northern Nigeria just then so we had to go to Lagos. It so happened that our visit coincided with the arrival from England of a Captain Rodd, (later Lord Rennell), on a special mission. Captain Rodd was looking for a senior district officer with army experience to set up a trans-frontier intelligence organisation in Kano, the commercial capital of Northern Nigeria and terminus of the old caravan routes. Bryan was in Lagos and he fitted. The Governor was approached and at once agreed to release him.

'I hear that you have a wife,' said Captain Rodd between pinches of snuff. 'She can be your Secretary.'

'I am sure my wife will be delighted to help, although she has had no secretarial training,' was the reply.

'She will soon learn,' said Captain Rodd.

Despite my complete lack of office experience, I was thrilled at the prospect of having a job and living in Kano. I had heard so much of its ancient walls, camels, and Arabs. Moreover, we planned to live inside the African city and not in the European suburb, three miles away. Bryan had at once written to the Resident to ask if the Emir would agree to our having the 'Gidan Shettima' and the reply was 'Yes.' This house was well over a hundred years old and had once been the residence of the envoy from the Court of Bornu, a powerful neighbouring kingdom bordering on Lake Chad and later a state in the Federation of Nigeria.

We flew back to Minna to pack once more. We had only been there six months. For four days the floor of the Residency was strewn with packing cases, straw and old newspapers. Usuman reverently lifted the antelope heads from their positions on the wall and placed each one in its own crate. He then folded my Bida curtains and packed them on top. Meanwhile, Tanko and I dealt with china, glass, gramophone records and pictures. At last, all was ready and we set forth by train for Kano.

4 KANO, SOKOTO, BORNU AND THE FRENCH CONNECTION

At six o'clock the next morning, our train steamed into Kano station. Looking through the carriage window, I saw a dense crowd of white-robed people against a background of dingy concrete. As we descended from the train, we were greeted by a high pitched buzz of flies, a mass of which were attracted to each one of us, whirring round our heads and trying to get into our mouths and eyes. As we drove away from the station, we thankfully shook them off.

Having breakfasted with one of Bryan's DO friends in a largely European suburb called Nassarawa, we set forth in steady rain to examine our new home, using our host's light lorry. As we approached the city, I had my first view of its famous wall. Thirty feet high and dusty pink in colour, it still encompassed the entire city, a distance of twelve miles. A goat had climbed its crumbling banks on one side of the gateway and was eyeing us as we mounted the ramp and passed through. Inside, was a vast honeycomb of flat-roofed mud buildings, interrupted here and there by open spaces and by two rocky hills. One of these, the Dallas rock was the place where the original settlers in Kano had lived. They were blacksmiths and they had chosen this rock for its iron content.

Our road was full of pot holes and we splashed along between gowned and turbanned cyclists. Several times we had to brake sharply to avoid sheep and donkeys which were wandering aimlessly across the highway. Many of the houses we passed were decorated with traditional patterns in bold bas-relief. Some had the date of construction and the owner's name on the front door. Then we entered a narrow alley, twisting between the houses. Finally, the road broadened again and on one side were municipal buildings in Moorish style, while on the other side, set back from the road and enclosed in a massive wall, was the Emir's palace. Two fierce old men in red and green gowns and scarlet turbans

31

guarded its arched entrance. We skirted the palace walls, turned several more bends and ended in another open space with crossroads in the middle and three large ponds at the corners. 'That's Gidan Shettima, over there!' said Bryan, pointing to the brink of the farthest pond where a domed roof just showed over a twenty-foot wall. To enter, we passed through a vaulted ante-room. This led to a courtyard which the rain had coverted into a lake of mud. I squelched my way carefully across. Entering the front door of the central building we found ourselves in a dark hall. Just visible at the end was an uneven stairway, winding upwards. To the right, an opening led into the main apartment, a lofty room with an arched ceiling reminding me of a village church. To the right again a door led into a low square room, which became the office. We returned to the living room and crossing to its opposite end found another small room, intended as a pantry. Through the back door and across the yard was the kitchen, a separate flat-roofed building. Years of smoke had blackened its inside walls, but at least it possessed a sink and a kitchen range. The servants' huts were attached to the back wall of the compound and as my eye caught two empty stables at one end of this row, I thought of my chestnut pony and Bryan's Sokoto black, which were being laboriously ridden up from Minna by their horse boys and were not expected for another fortnight.

We returned to the house to explore the upper storey. It consisted of just one bedroom, very low and narrow. A little light filtered in beneath a half open shutter, for Gidan Shettima had no glass windows. Nor was their a bath. Instead, at one end of the bedroom floor was a cement slab with an outlet at one corner and a shower bath rose hanging from above.

The rain had practically stopped by this time, so we ventured outside to explore the roof. The lower level, which faced inwards, became our dry season sleeping place and we were very glad of it, for the narrow room inside was stifling in hot weather. The high level beside the dome, which we approached by a rickety wooden staircase with many steps missing, became our sitting out place at night. It had a splendid view of the city, across the Mosque towards the Emir's Palace. As the old Mosque had fallen down and the new one had yet to be built, an area of hallowed ground was used instead, marked off by a low wall. At prayer times we could see the faithful engaged in their devotions. They stood in rows facing the east. First, having completed their ceremonial ablutions, they pushed the wide sleeves of their gowns back over their shoulders, then swung their arms, murmuring words of praise. Finally, all together and in perfect rhythm, they bowed themselves to the ground, touching the earth with their foreheads. I found it an inspiring sight. I was used to seeing individual Muslims saying their prayers, for unlike Christians, they performed their devotions in public without the slightest self-consciousness at the five appointed times a day. The prayer was an act of total submission. the only occasion when the community as a whole assembled in the Great Mosque was on Fridays at *azuhur*, that is at about two o'clock in the afternoon. Smaller Mosques and prayer grounds, marked out with stones, were used at other times. Usuman, who was a convert from Paganism and very devout, used to say his prayers at the back of the compound, using his sheep-skin prayer mat.

Allah seemed to enter into everyting and the more Hausa I learnt, the more I found myself unconsciously adopting Muslim ways of speech. If told of a death, for instance, one learnt to say 'Allah have mercy on him,' while 'if possible' became 'if Allah wills' and, in response to the Hausa 'Goodnight' literally 'Till the morning', one said 'Allah bring us safely!' Soon, the cracked but penetrating tones of the muezzi calling the faithful to prayer from the minaret, became one of our more familiar noises. The first call of *'Allahu Akbar-r-r'* (God is great) woke us each morning just before dawn, or 'as soon as a black thread could be distinguished from a white one,' to use the Muslim definition.

To return to Gidan Shettima: to have our staircase mended was our first task, then we had to acquire some furniture. All that we found on arrival were two upright chairs, one table and a hospital bedstead. This had been used by a doctor from the City Hospital, the last occupant of the house. The difficulty was that, as a politico-military organisation, we belonged neither to the administration, nor wholly to the army. From the point of view of furniture for our 'quarters', neither would own us. Fortunately, Bryan had many friends in the Public Works Department and a little charm of manner did the trick. The next day a lorry load of furniture arrived, including sorely needed shelves and tables and a set of rather uncomfortable verandah chairs. The army provided us with office equipment and a handsome navy blue three ton truck, chosen especially for us by Captain Rodd.

The antelope heads were then carefully unpacked and fixed on the walls, while my Bida curtains were strung across the windows on makeshift pieces of wire. The effect was not unattractive. The village church had become an old world baronial hall.

More important than furnishings, however, was the office staff. First to join the 'Research Office', as our organisation was ambiguously christened, was Frank Humphreys, an able Irishman with a dry sense of humour. The next addition, L.C. Giles was a brilliant linguist whose attractive Swiss wife also helped. Our next task was to find four messengers with knowledge of the border areas to act as agents. Three were old friends of Bryan's, stalwart Hausas like the Umaru we had left in Minna. The fourth, named 'Arab', although a stranger to us, was well known to Captain Rodd. His name was misleading for he was in fact a Tuareg. His eyes were hazel and his skin not much browner than a European's might be if he spent his life in the tropical sun. His features were almost Nordic. He spoke Hausa with a slow foreign accent and his manner was gentle and aloof. For some reason, he had ceased to wear the veil behind which Tuaregs normally conceal their faces. Captain Rodd's acquaintance with these strange nomads dated back to his two journeys of exploration in the Southern Sahara in 1922 and 1927. Crossing the desert by camel and living close to the people, he had acquired an intimate knowledge of their language, customs and history as shown in his book *People of the Veil*. Before leaving the desert, he gave his two Tuareg guides a Maria Theresa dollar with a large segment removed. He told them that if they ever received the missing fragment, they should accompany the bearer to wherever he told them. Captain Rodd gave Bryan the missing piece, which he sent to Agadez, near where these men lived, Agadez being an important French centre in the Colonie du Niger and a focal point of the main trans-Saharan caravan routes. Eventually the two men arrived at Gidan Shettima and provided the Research Office with much useful information.

Captain Rodd lived with us at Gidan Shettima whenever he visited Kano, staying in a separate building attached to the front wall. It was even more like a village church than our hall. He had it re-decorated, with the arches picked out in mushroom pink. Unfortunately, he did not have much opportunity of enjoying his room, nor we his stimulating conversation. He was obliged to divide his time between his Lagos and Kano offices and as soon as both were functioning smoothly, he left Nigeria. We continued to see him from time to time when he passed through Kano airport en route for some other part of Africa. He rose in rank with bewildering speed and in a matter of months had become a Major General.

To return to the staff of Gidan Shettima, there was no clerk nor secretary apart from me, a complete novice. Captain Rodd and

Bryan had to be patient until by practice I had acquired some speed and accuracy as a typist. I was given lessons in filing and card indexing and in such spare time as remained I absorbed a book on office management by a DO named Niven (later Sir Rex Niven). Codes and cyphers then had to be mastered and finally I had to improve my French for one of our duties was to interview all French officers escaping from Vichy territory into Nigeria to join the forces of General de Gaulle.

There were, of course, British as well as French guests to entertain and these included the Area Commander from Lagos. The day after he arrived on his first visit, he asked me to take him to see Kano market. I began at the witch doctor's ju-ju stall, where remedies for every ailment known to man were displayed. These included the leg and front of a hyena, human bones and collections of vulture's feathers. The general seemed very set on buying me some antimony, a blue-black powder used locally as eye shadow. We soon came to the sword and saddlery department, where he found the ancient salesman more interesting than his wares. With a little persuasion, the sword merchant was induced to wave a spear defiantly in the air, while unbeknownst, the general took his photograph. We moved on followed by a rabble of inquisitive children and disappointed traders, carrying rejected wares and a selection of other goods dug up from behind their stalls. Earthenware pots, grass baskets, rolls of cloth, skins and saddles were carried head high in their motley procession. In the end, the general bought a calabash ornamented with poker work, some red beads and two string baskets.

Not long after the Area Commander's visit, networks of telephone wires and wireless aerials were installed into Gidan Shettima and a British NCO with four African wireless operators were added to the staff. They and their apparatus occupied what had once been Captain Rodd's room.

Bryan was known to his friends in Kano at this time rather teasingly as 'S.S. and Hush-Hush'. They regarded the Research Office as something of a joke. Perhaps this was just as well for it enabled him to carry on his secret organisation without serious scrutiny. He himself would have been the first to admit that some of his devices were like something out of a spy story. Once, I walked into the office and found him carefully pasting a message on a wine bottle.

'What on earth are you doing?' I asked.

Without replying, he picked up the wine merchant's lable which he had just steamed off, and stuck it back on to the bottle by its edges, covering the message.

'Sending a letter to Zinder,' he said at last.

Zinder was the Vichy military headquarters, nearly two hundred miles north of Kano.

'Oh, but surely you don't expect it to get through the frontier guards?'

'Well, I intend to try,' he insisted.

The message did reach its destination and after an anxious interval of five weeks, we received a reply. By this and other devices, the Research Office built up a picture of what was going on the other side of the frontier.

Fortunately for us, our Vichy French neighbours, though hostile at times, were not aggressive. They were agents of a dispirited regime which, having just themselves swallowed the bitter pill of defeat, resented our continuance of the fight. To add to their dislike of us, based on wounded national pride, the Nazis fed them skilfully with anti-British propaganda. The British and Free French attacks on Oran and Dakar provided excellent material for stories of alleged Allied atrocities. Their trump card was a film given wide circulation throughout French West Africa which appeared to show British airmen firing on defenceless Vichy sailors as they floundered in the water. But this happened later. Meanwhile, the more we learnt of conditions on the other side, the more we realised how substantial and well equipped their forces were compared with ours. Fortunately, although Vichy had its own intelligence organisation in the area using African traders as agents, we doubted whether they were aware of our weakness. In fact, what they most seemed to fear was an attack from our side of the frontier.

For former friends and allies to be spying on one another would have been a sorry state of affairs, had Vichy represented the majority opinion in French West Africa. But this was far from being the case. There were many bitterly opposed to the Pétainist regime, determined to continue the fight and restore honour and freedom to their country. Some succeeded in escaping into Allied territory, others tried but were caught and shot by the Vichy frontier guards. Of those who were successful were two Camel Corps captains named Despian and Langlois. They were our first visitors at Gidan Shettima from across the border. Regular officers from families with an army tradition, they did not regret the action they had just taken, yet felt keenly unhappy at having left their units in the desert. We listened to their story in the 'baronial hall', gave them drinks and did our best to make them feel that they were amongst friends. The next morning they departed for the Free French territory of the French Cameroons. Almost at once, they joined an expedition to capture the Vichy-controlled territory of Gabon, which submitted to the Free French after a short skirmish on the beaches, but, tragically, Despian was killed. Langlois returned to Kano about six months later as Free French liaison officer with our office and with the Nigeria Regiment. A handsome, young man with a fresh complexion and dark eyes, he became extremely popular with the British community in Kano, where he remained for about a year. Then to his joy, he was sent to the Free French Territory of Chad to join General Leclerc's Motorised Column which later crossed the Sahara by a long and arduous route and joined the Eighth Army at the Mareth line.

Soon after saying 'Goodbye' to these two brave Frenchmen, we left for our first tour of the north west frontier. Touring the border areas was an important part of our work, the object being to pick up information from the local native administration (NA) officials and from the many villagers who were still clandestinely trading across the frontier. The kind of intelligence we needed was about troop movements, the state of the roads, economic conditions and the morale of the Vichy French. This time there was a special object about which more will be told later.

Using the three-ton truck, we jolted our way 350 miles north west of Sokoto. At first, we passed through flat farmlands dotted with baobab trees, portly, gnarled and grotesque. Villages were frequent and we passed through and stopped at several sizable towns. After the first hundred miles, however, the park-like country changed into arid scrub. In several places, bush fires raged so close to the road that I feared the lorry might explode. For long stretches we saw no living creatures but crown birds and hornbills which rose lethargically into the air as our truck trundled along. Six miles before we reached our destination, the dry bush ceased and we found ourselves on rolling downs overlooking the Sokoto River valley. For a moment I was reminded of the Cotswolds.

Conrad Williams, an old friend of Bryan's, had asked us to stay with him. He was the district officer in charge of Sokoto's finances. We had some difficulty in finding his bungalow, but after being given directions by a helpful native administrative policeman, we eventually drove up to his front door. We must have looked a couple of frights. Our faces were thickly coated with red dust thrown up from the road and my hair had been blown into dry strands, for the intense heat had made my headscarf unbearable. Conrad welcomed us charmingly and showed not the slightest surprise at our appearance. We were soon washed, changed and gratefully sipping cool drinks. Helen, Conrad's American fiancée, was also staying in Sokoto.

The following day, a north-east wind from the desert, locally known as the 'harmattan', enveloped Sokoto in a mist of fine dust. The tree at the bottom of Conrad's garden was scarcely visible and the sun shone through feebly, like a lemon balloon. This haze looked like an English fog, but instead of feeling clammy, it was harsh and stinging. Frequent applications of salve did not prevent our lips from cracking. The mist cleared a little as the day progressed and after lunch the sun was hot enough for us all to feel like a siesta. For that afternoon, Helen and I shared a bedroom. After a year in an austere, hardworking male atmosphere, I enjoyed discussing novels and fashions and 'Taking the back hair down' with another young woman.

We both rode, so the next morning, which was a Sunday, Helen and myself, with five or six other young people, were cantering across the sandy wastes which surrounded Sokoto. But for the ridges of corn stubble one would never have guessed that this was farmland in the rains. Here and there, we passed groups of round mud houses where apiky acacias and tamarind trees gave meagre shade. After two miles, we came to the Forest Reserve, where rows of neem trees, originally imported from India, miraculously flourished and grew green leaves. The ponies enjoyed the coolness and bounded forward whenever we turned a bend. On our way back, we passed through another 'oasis', Sokoto Gardens. These had been laid out by an imaginative medical officer in the earliest years of British occupation. A brown stream trickled through the valley, flanked by green grass and flower beds. Beyond the lawns were mahogany trees of great height. In one short avenue, their upper branches intertwined, making arches. As our ponies rustled the leaves underfoot, Helen told me that they called this place the 'cathedral'. Presently we passed the Club, a thatched building on a terrace hung with flowers.

During this day, Bryan and the three-ton truck departed for a frontier town. When they returned, there was a report to write so I ceased being frivolous and returned to work with my typewriter.

Bryan and I took an evening stroll and once again I was charmed by the courtliness of the people we met along the road. Each one stopped and said, 'Greetings to you, Master, how have you spent the day?' and when Bryan made the customary reply of 'Quite well,' the salutation was repeated, word for word, to me.

The following day, the Sultan of Sokoto came to call accompanied by his Council. A procession of cars arrived, similar but rather longer than the one I had seen in Kontagora. Helen and I moved into another room, but when the official business was over, we were invited to meet the Sultan and his Council and to exchange greetings. We all sat for a few minutes, Conrad having motioned the Sultan towards the settee. The Council preferred to sit on the floor in their chief's presence. The Sultan was a simple, gracious, man, lightly built and of medium height. He wore a white turban and robe and an olive green kaftan. There was a friendliness and humour in his eyes and an effortless authority in his manner. He was more than a temporal chief of a large emirate – for he had the special title of 'Commander of the Faithful', which meant that his spiritual influence extended to most Muslims in a large part of West Africa.

When the Sultan and the Waziri, his chief councillor, were together they were not in the least pompous, but full of wit and gaiety. The Waziri was a much older man with aquiline features. He was the Sultan's constant companion and partner in repartee, though the Waziri always preserved the right degree of deference. Many were the stories they told of their adventures in London when they stayed at the Hyde Park Hotel. The arrival of these robed and turbanned dignitaries from Nigeria must have caused surprise enough, even in those days. Imagine the astonishment of the waiter when the Waziri, finding his soup too hot, ordered ice cream to cool it. The Waziri interpolated his stories with such respectful exclamations to the Sultan as 'May your life be lengthened!' and 'God give you luck!' It was a sad day for Sokoto and for us too when this lively and forceful old man was laid to his rest ten years later. His younger brother replaced him.

Amongst other member of the Council was the Sardauna, a distant cousin of the Sultan. A tall, well-built man with smiling eyes, he too had charm rivalling that of his exalted kinsman.

The only councillor who looked out of place sitting on the floor was the *Alkalin Alkalai*, literally the 'Judge of Judges'. Perhaps this was because his impressive smile and serene manner marked him so plainly as a dignitary of the law. His title implied that he was chief judge of the Muslim courts of Sokoto Emirate. These courts tried almost all civil and criminal cases. The Chief Alkali's Court was the most important for it dealt with the more serious cases and heard appeals from lower courts in the outlying districts. Cases affecting Europeans and those which were for some other reason unsuitable for Muslim Courts were tried by a magistrate under English law. The magistrate was usually also the district officer, except in the main towns.

To return to the Sultan's councillors. Each had his own responsibilities in the local government. One was in charge of schools, another public works and so on. They were very far from being a body of ceremonial 'Yes-men'. Collectively, they were known as the 'Native Administration' or the NA for short.

After the guests had gone, Conrad explained that the Sultan was a direct descendant and successor of the great leader of the Fulani Rebellion, Usuman dan Fodio.

'Oh yes,' I said, 'I heard of him in Kontagora, where the Emir is also a descendant. But what caused this rebellion?'

Bryan explained that it really began as a dispute between Usuman dan Fodio and the Hausa King of Gobir. That is a country north west of Sokoto. Dan Fodio was a Muslim scholar and teacher and very popular amongst his own people. The Hausa had been converted to Islam many centuries before, but they had become slack about their religion and pagan practices were creeping back. The King of Gobir himself had completely reverted to heathenism. Usuman dan Fodio preached reform and return to the true faith and his influence grew so strong that the King was alarmed and threw some of the Muslims into prison in a vain attempt to assert his authority. When Usuman dan Fodio forcibly freed the captives, the rising started. Under his inspiring leadership, the revolt spread like a forest fire. To the Fulani, it was a holy war. They were like champions of the true faith, converting or killing the infidel wherever they went. They ended by conquering an enormous area, covering most of what is now Northern Nigeria and overlapping well into Niger Colony and Dahomey in French territory, now both independent states.

I asked whether the Fulani regarded Usuman dan Fodio as their great national hero and Bryan replied, 'Very much so, in fact they consider him a saint and every year many hundreds of people from all over the country visit his tomb.'

5A FESTIVAL AND A POLISH ODYSSEY

The next day was the greater of the two main festivals of the Islamic year, known in Hausa as the *"Babban Salla."* To Muslims it was Christmas and Easter rolled into one. Everyone, to the smallest child, had smart new clothes and feasting and visiting of friends lasted for several days. The earlier *"Salla"*, although less important, was in a sense more dramatic in that it marked the end of the fast month of Ramadan. During the whole of this period, no one except expectant mothers and young children might eat, drink or even rinse the mouth between sunrise and sunset, stern discipline in so hot and dry a climate. Large meals were cooked and consumed during the hours of darkness, people talked and drums throbbed all night, with the result that no one had much sleep. During the day, servants wilted and it was no use trying to keep up the usual standards of household efficiency. I had to restrain myself from allowing my finger to run too often along dusty shelves and table. One of my staff had severe migraines during the first two weeks, before he had 'got into training'. At the close of Ramadan in every village and town, crowds gathered watching the western horizon just after sunset for some sign of the new moon. There was great relief and rejoicing when its thin delicate outline was seen, proclaiming that the fast was ended and the feast would take place next day. Sometimes, clouds or mist obscured it. Then the Sultan waited for news from elsewhere, for as 'Commander of the Faithful' it was for him to make the pronouncement. As a rule, news of the moon's appearance arrived by telegram or telephone, but if no such tidings were forthcoming, the fast continued. At both *Salla* feasts, religious ceremonies, led by the emirs took place at every town and, as a rule, Europeans and other non-Muslim guests were invited to watch the spectacle.

On the morning of the Great Salla of Sokoto, we were all dressed and outside Conrad's bungalow at eight o'clock. The district officers were in high-necked, white drill uniforms, with gilt

41

buttons and black gorgettes, trimmed with gold. For trousers, they wore tight white overalls fastened beneath black wellington boots by patent leather straps, making it quite impossible to bend at the knee. Their faces were heavily shaded by white Wolseley helmets, on the front of which gleamed a Royal Coat of Arms. Bryan for once was spared having to wear this uncomfortable dress, since he was in army uniform. Helen and I were wearing our best dresses, picture hats and gloves. The cars, specially polished for the occasion, were standing by when Conrad, who had been consulting his watch from time to time, decided that the right moment had come, we all climbed in and drove towards the city. On reaching the gates, we took a circular route which skirted the town. This led to the *Wurin Idi* or praying place outside the city walls, which was set apart from these two festivals. On the way, we passed a group of excited little girls in colourful silks, wearing silver bangles, necklaces and earrings. Older women, similarly attired, peeped over the walls of their houses. Meanwhile, their menfolk hastened to the place of prayer. I noticed one or two very small boys, not more than five years old, wearing grown up gowns and embroidered skull caps. They kept on pushing back floppy sleeves over small bony shoulders, as they toddled along trying desperately to keep up with their older relations.

Presently, our cars left the motor road for a rough track which curved down to the *Wurin Idi* where already a large crowd had collected. A row of chairs had been prepared for European spectators a few yards from the assembly. We took our places. Meanwhile, a steady shuffle of hooves announced the beginning of the procession. There were robes of embroidered homespun, rich silks and satins studded with sequins, and colours ranging from pastel pink to peacock green and scarlet. Turbans, standing stiff and high, were of spotted muslin, yellow tulle and shiny beaten indigo. Richly-caparisoned horses stepped proudly forward, their nodding heads rustling the ornaments. Then I saw a solitary Arab in a gap in the procession, towering above the horsemen on a long-stepping white camel. Next came the Sultan's personal body guard. There was chain mail, so old that from a distance it looked like lace, and plumed helmets recalling the crusades. Finally, through the mist, we saw the slim young figure of the Sultan, in the centre of a close group of horsemen. He was clad from head to foot in white since, as leader of the faith, he must dress and behave with utmost dignity and simplicity. A one-time slave walked beside him, carrying an enormous multi-coloured umbrella, which he rotated above his master's head. The Sultan was helped to dismount, then made his way through the centre of the congregation and was soon out of sight. There was a hush, broken only by the whinny of horses tethered in the background. The worshippers swung their arms, bowed to the ground, murmured prayers and bowed again. We could not see the ram which was tethered in the midst of the congregation awaiting slaughter, but a sigh from the crowd signalled the moment of sacrifice. Presently, the Sultan reappeared and walked towards the guests. A seat with an embroidered velvet rug thrown over it had been prepared for him, opposite the Resident's chair. We all rose while greetings were exchanged. He sat for a moment. Then, rising once more, walked down the line of guests, talking to each one. As he approached us, I was struck by the uplifted look on his face. He returned to his horse and mounted, and there were shouts of 'God give you life'. Drummers on horseback and musicians with six-foot trumpets together produced a blaring, throbbing accompaniment. The umbrella was once more set in motion and the procession receded gradually into the mist.

Taking a different route in our cars, we arrived first at the Sultan's palace. We were led upstairs to a balcony above the main entrance. Soon, the beginning of the procession could be seen winding towards the palace. At last, the Sultan arrived with a group of retainers, and joined us on the balcony at the centre of which a throne had been prepared for him. From there he addressed his people. The speech finished, there were prolonged acclamations from the crowd. Various entertainments followed including exhibitions of wrestling and comic turns by the court jester, who wore a long-haired wig and costume. Eventually, the Resident took leave of the Sultan and we all returned to our houses.

A lesser personality of Sokoto, yet one who seemed an essential character, was the snake charmer. We did not meet him on the first visit, but on the following occasion, when we were staying at the rest house, the snake man came to see us. He stood patiently under a locust bean tree waiting to be noticed. We called him and he came towards us, stopping at a safe distance. Then he produced from a large calabash a python, two cobras and a viper which coiled round his arms and shoulders, swinging their heads back and forth. Having replaced the snakes, he drew from his pockets five or six scorpions which walked up and down his bare brown arms, threshing the air with their poison-tipped tails. Finally, we tossed him a few shillings and said 'Goodbye till we come again'.

Snake charmers had practical as well as entertainment value. If a snake was seen disappearing into a dark corner of a house, or, as often happened, into a thatched roof, for a small fee a charmer would lure it out by sprinkling the area where it had appeared with seemingly magic powders.

On our fourth visit to Sokoto, staying as before at the rest house, we looked in vain under the familiar tree for our friend. By the next day there was still no sign of him so Bryan sent Usuman to the town to make enquiries. He came back with the news that the snake charmer had just died, killed by one of his own snakes. His son took over the business and later came to give us a display. He was very expensively dressed, quite different from his modest father.

Now for the principal object of our tour. We had been called to Sokoto to investigate the story of five Poles who, escaping from the Germans and wishing to continue the fight with the allies, had crossed into Nigeria from Vichy territory at the South West corner of Sokoto Province. Only the leader's wife spoke a little English and they had tried to tell their extremely complicated story to the Resident in French. Were they genuine or a set of clever spies? The Resident was perplexed, but on the whole he believed them. The party consisted of a regular cavalry officer with a close-shaved head and his neat, dark wife; a territorial major who had a farm in Morocco with a fair, flamboyant wife and finally, a Polish NCO who acted as chauffeur-mechanic. In a couple of small Citreon cars, they had crossed the Sahara, ostensibly destined for Vichy French Dahomey. Having passed a point on the road within five miles of Nigeria, they made the excuse of having left a suitcase behind at the previous night's rest camp, doubled back and then branched down a disused track which friends had told them led to the Nigerian frontier. In many places the track was overgrown by bush and they were continually held up to cut away undergrowth or remove rocks, fearing all the time that they might be followed. At last they crossed into Nigeria and Allied territory. Bryan held a series of interviews with them and gradually built up the picture. First of all, he asked for their passports. The cavalry officer's wife replied, 'We each have two passports, one genuine, one faked. Do you wish to see both?' Bryan replied that she and her companions had better tell him the whole story right from the start.

The cavalry officer's wife explained that in 1939 the country was invaded by the Germans from the west and the Russians from the east. Her husband was with the Armoured Division. She was alone in their home in the country. Before long, the Russians arrived. They requistioned the house, occupied and terrorised their village. School children were forced to betray their parents. People disappeared at dead of night. She was homeless and unhappy and did not know what to do. Then she heard that her husband and many of his unit had escaped into France. It so happened that she had a friend who was the wife of another officer in her husband's unit. Together, they planned to escape into France too. First of all they arranged for passports to be faked. Then they dressed in thick gloves and boots and all the clothes they could carry. They made their way first into Czechoslovakia, then, crossing a high range of mountains through snow and intense cold, reached Hungary. The next objective was Yugoslavia. Walking and hitch-hiking, the journey took many months. Fortunately, they had friends both in Hungary and Yugoslavia. When at last they reached the South of France, they went to live in Marseilles, seeking news of their husbands. Weeks passed and she said if she had not been 'a believer' (croyante) she thought she would have given up hope. Then there came an incredible stroke of luck. She walked straight into her husband in a street in Marseilles. By this time France had collapsed. Her husband naturally wanted to continue to fight. Somehow they had to find their way into Allied territory. To reach England was impossible. It so happened that her husband had a friend, another major in his unit, who owned a farm in North Africa, not far from Casablanca. If they reached there, it might be possible to continue the journey across Africa until they reached British territory. After some delay, the Vichy authorities granted the necessary passes. Sailing for Algiers, they then made their way to the friend's farm, where his wife was living. These friends decided to sell their property and with the proceeds they bought equipment for the journey across the Sahara and these two cars. Now they wanted to go to Egypt where they believed that a Polish Brigade was forming. They asked for help.

The Poles gave much useful information about the desert routes from the point of view of armoured vehicles. Surprisingly, after their long and arduous journey the party arrived in Nigeria in excellent health. They all had a healthy tan and the wives, who had only two dresses each, always managed to look fresh and well groomed. They accompanied us back to Kano and I drove one of their Citreons some of the way. Having reached Kano, they naturally wanted to continue their journey as soon as possible, but their story had to be checked by higher authority before permission to leave Nigeria could be granted and, even then, they still had to wait for sea passages to the Middle East. They found this delay very trying. The cavalry major spent some of his time riding and playing polo with British officers and they all devoted much effort to learning English. After they had left, we often wondered what happened to this brave and determined little party. The only news we ever had of them was on a postcard sent from Alexandria.

By this time, Christmas was approaching and I began to plan my plum puddings. The Emir of Kano had several times sent us presents of 'alkhaki' and other cakes made by his Arab cook. In return, I thought of sending him one of my puddings. I consulted Bryan. 'Do you think he will really enjoy it?' Bryan's reply was that he would certainly appreciate the gesture and might even eat some himself provided some reliable witness assured him that nothing 'Haram' (forbidden) had been included. So two reliable Muslims, both messengers, were posted in the kitchen to watch preparations. I chose the fruitarian recipe from Mrs Beeton. Hardly any of the ingredients were available, so I used local substitutes; wild honey for golden syrup, ground nuts for almonds, dates for currants and raisins, green paw paw for apples. Alcohol and anything derived from the pig, such as lard, were, of course, taboo. At last the Emir's pudding was ready. I packed it with Christmas wrappers and ribbon and sent it over. A polite word of thanks was returned and I still wonder if he touched it. Modesty prevented his mentioning it during the course of our next conversation.

He did however consent to have tea with us one day. He rode from his palace on a white mule, surrounded by courtiers and preceded by the court flatterer, who sang out the customary words of praise. Trailing along behind was the usual following of admiring adults and inquisitive children. The Emir dismounted and was escorted through the porch into Gidan Shettima. Conversation at tea time was confined to greetings and conventional topics. The Emir was very reserved and we did not want to embarrass him. Perhaps he felt nervous too, for I had noticed that he had a marked tremor in his right hand. Occasionally, his face was lit by a half-hidden smile.

We literally lived in the office which overflowed into the sitting-room and, as far as I was concerned, the bedroom as well. I used to take my codes and cypher apparatus there in the afternoons when I was having my so-called 'siesta'. Bryan and Frank would work late into the night and we were not infrequently woken in the early hours by Most Immediate telegrams. As they were almost invariably in cypher, I had to throw off the fog of sleep and set to work with the rest. If the message revealed a 'flap' (war-time slang for 'emergency') Bryan used to spend the remaining hours of darkness 'taking action', while I gratefully returned to bed.

When the pressure of work slackened, we occasionally went to Kano's open air cinema. This consisted of an elevated concrete screen, which looked like an enormous hoarding, facing which the audience were accommodated in rows of dilapidated canvas chairs, which sagged in the middle of the back, just where one most needed support. To make matters worse, the prevailing wind brought with it a sickening stench from a near-by hides and skins yard. During the harmattan, it was so cold that Bryan wore his British warm and I my English overcoat and we wrapped a rug round our knees. Despite these discomforts, we enjoyed the films but had the greatest difficulty in keeping awake.

For exercise, I used to ride each morning before breakfast. This meant negotiating a mile of narrow alleys through a densely populated area before emerging by one of the city gates, into the open country. As in Sokoto, passers-by were friendly and courteous although at first they seemed surprised to see a white woman alone and on horseback. Only once was there an incident. I was riding up the narrow slope which led to one of the city gates when a young horseman, to have some fun and amuse his friends, charged straight at me, halting his horse in a flurry of dust only a few feet in front of me. My pony reared and side-stepped and I very nearly fell sideways into a foul and stony ditch. When the story reached the ears of the Ciroma, the Emir's favourite and most influential son, he was angry and had the young horseman reprimanded.

On our first Christmas morning in Gidan Shettima we had another unexpected guest from across the frontier. This was a Frenchman named Genin. After the defeat of France, pretending to support Petain, he had continued working with the Germans at Vichy clinking glasses of champagne with them, collaborating, but all the time memorising every important piece of information. Then he feigned a breakdown in health and asked leave to visit his brother on the Ivory Coast. This was granted and he made his way to North Africa, crossing the Sahara as far as the desert town of Gao on the banks of the River Niger. Then instead of continuing his journey to the Ivory Coast, he boarded an African trader's canoe which was heading downstream to Gaya, close to the north west corner of Nigeria. The journey took fourteen days during which Genin had to remain completely concealed, for he felt certain that by this time the Vichy authorities would be searching for him. He was almost smothered by his coverings and eaten alive by fleas and mosquitoes. When the canoe reached its destination, Genin remained hidden till nightfall, then following the same track as the Poles had taken a few months before, made his way into Nigeria. Fortunately, it was a dark night or he might not have eluded the vigilance of the frontier guards, who were watching this escape route and had been specially selected for their anti-British and anti-Gaullist sympathies.

Once over the border, Genin found friendly Africans who directed him to the nearest motor road. Here, a passing lorry driver gave him a lift to Sokoto. The Resident arranged transport to take him to the Research Office at Kano. It was not until he was under the roof at Gidan Shettima that he was able to tell his story, which was a great relief for him for, as he said, 'my lips have been sealed for so long.'

The following day was Boxing Day. We asked Genin if he would care to join us at the festivities at Kano Club, but he refused. 'I have no heart for such things. I think of my wife and four children in Brittany. They have very little to eat and who knows what the Boche will do to them now that they know of my escape?'

About this time, rumours were circulating in Nigeria of either an attempted invasion of England by the Germans or a full-scale invasion rehearsal which had ended in disaster. There were stories of scores of charred corpses washed up on the Channel coasts of England and France and of hundreds of badly burned German soldiers being cared for under conditions of extreme secrecy. The story was that large numbers of invasion barges had been surprised by the Royal Air Force which had dropped petrol on the surrounding sea and had then set light to it. Genin, who was in the Deuxieme Bureau at the time, reported that this story had wide circulation and considerable credence in Vichy France even in quite responsible circles and that it had greatly strengthened French morale. News that this story was current in France as well as in Nigeria made it seem that there must be something in it and so helped our morale as well. Genin was killed not many months later by Vichy forces in the Syrian campaign.

6 FREE FRENCH, GENERAL DE GAULLE, AND VICHY FRENCH

We made two tours to Bornu in the north-eastern corner of Nigeria. The first was in February, the second, and more extensive, in May. The intention was to make enquiries about conditions the other side of the frontier as close as possible to the north east border of the Province. This meant making first for Maiduguri, the capital of Bornu, about 350 miles from Kano. Then we planned to follow a series of bush tracks marked on our map by uncertain dotted lines. They ran north-east from Maiduguri, parallel and quite close to Lake Chad. We were unlikely to see this vast inland sea, which bordered partly on Vichy territory and partly on Free French territory, for a wide stretch of reedy swamp masked its Nigerian shore. However, we hoped to catch a glimpse of some elephants, for several herds were known to live in the area through which we would be passing.

The army, in its inscrutable way, had removed our three-ton truck and replaced it by a desert-yellow contraption known as the 'Safari Wagon'. It was a cross between an estate car and the larger size in Land Rovers and, for long distance travel, it was certainly less uncomfortable than the lorry. Its one disadvantage was that the stream of dust thrown up by its front wheels seemed to be directed straight at the passengers' faces. The servants, with unconscious humour, called it the 'Suffering Wagon'.

Arab was an expert on Bornu, known now more correctly as 'Borno', having served there as a government messenger for many years, so we took him as an interpreter and guide. With him were our usual domestic staff and in addition, a new driver who came to us with the safari wagon. He was a rather self-confident young man whose experiences of driving had been largely confined to tarmac roads in the shady forest lands of Southern Nigeria. He had one or two surprises awaiting him in northern Bornu's burning wastes.

Our loads consisted of ample supplies of camp equipment, provisions for three weeks and plenty of drinks, May being the

49

hottest month of the year. We made sure this time that we were well weighed down. On the last occasion, we had been unwise enough to travel with the three-ton truck almost empty and the rapid succession of bumps and jolts caused by pot holes, patches of sand and hidden rocks had given us both headaches and made our insides feel as though reduced to jelly. After the first sixty miles we had called a halt for the night and subsided exhausted into deck chairs. When we had both recovered a little, Bryan fixed up our travelling wireless and to our joy we heard news of Wavell's first victory on the Western Desert.

To return to our second visit to Bornu. Having the safari wagon, we certainly travelled more comfortably. The road improved after half way, but as luck would have it, we stopped for lunch at a wayside rest house where a DO had shot himself. The caretaker followed us around, despite discouragement, telling us the story of the tragedy in lurid detail. We swallowed our sandwiches hastily and with little relish and were soon on our way to Maiduguri, where we arrived in time for a late cup of tea. Rex Niven, the acting resident, was an authority on the history of Bornu and the author of several books about Nigeria, and also of my *Guide to Office Management*. He had invited us to stay. He was not living in the Residency, but in the Senior District Officer's quarter, a new, two-storeyed house, smaller than the Residency but more convenient. The Residency stood importantly on the crest of a hill. It looked like a castle. Temporarily it was occupied by Free French airmen and the tricolour flew at the flagpole. I doubt if they enjoyed their stay at the Residency very much since it was infested with stink bugs, scaly grey beetles with an unpleasantly sweet odour. At harvest time each year they emerged from amongst the crops and literally took possession of the house, crawling slowly along shelves and tables in their legions and even clinging to the walls and ceilings. Spraying with insecticides, fumigation and swatting had all been tried in vain. Rex's predecessor once had a 'blitz' on them and an accumulation weighing over a ton was swept up and burnt, but by the next season, fresh beetles had arrived and had re-taken possession. In the end, the Residency had to be demolished and rebuilt on a different site.

After tea, Rex told me something of the history of the strong and independent Kingdom of Bornu, which had been famous as far back as the Middle Ages. In the early nineteenth century Bornu had successfully thrown back Usuman dan Fodio's invading armies. Even to that day, few Fulani had ventured to bring their cattle into the province, the nomadic herdsmen being mainly Shuwa Arabs. The settled people and its rulers were Kanuri, men of powerful build who carried swords as normally as British city men carry their furled umbrellas. For Muslims, the women had unusual independence and were said to be heavy spenders on dress. Their costume was like a kimono, with panels of different colours and it was fashionable to stain the teeth and gums a bright orange with the juice of the tobacco flower. Their hair styles fascinated me, the most common being a mass of tightly curled plaits which radiated from the top of the head like the spokes of a half-shut umbrella.

The ruler of Bornu was called the 'Shehu' (pronounced Shay-hoo). He was aged and nearly blind but still much held in awe. He spoke neither English nor Hausa and as few British officers knew more than a smattering of Kanuri, an unusually difficult language, conversation was carried on through interpreters. This meant that there could rarely be the same close sympathy as existed between many of the Fulani and Hausa emirs and their British administrators.

That night was hot and breathless. We slept outside on the guest room balcony and when the sun rose, before six a.m., much earlier than at Kano, being farther east, it shone brazenly upon us as we lay in bed awaiting our early morning cup of tea.

By midday, the mercury on Rex's maximum and minimum thermometer, which hung in his shady car porch, was registering 115°F, a record for that season. Our next day's journey was to take us to higher temperatures still, so we resolved to make a really early start.

We were up long before the sun had risen. In fact, it was only just peeping over the horizon as we drove through Maiduguri's broad, dusty high street. (Maiduguri has since been transformed by the planting of thousands of shady neem trees.) Turning north, we left the town by a rough track, demarcated by a straggling hedge of some reed-like succulent. At first, we passed through derelict farms where everything was bone dry and the odd cactus bush and spiky acacia were the only signs of life. In several places, owing to patches of deep sand, cars had abandoned the road and formed subsidiary tracks on either side.

After the first ten miles, the trouble started. Noticing an approaching dip in the road, Bryan yelled from the back, 'Get into bottom . . . quick!' But our driver was too late. The engine roared like several pneumatic drills while the wheels spun around without gripping, but lowering us deeper and deeper into the sand. At last he stopped the engine, which was issuing forth clouds of steam, and jumped out, but the moment his bare feet touched the burning earth he gave a yelp of pain and fell onto the sand. The rest of the staff collapsed with unsympathetic laughter. They had all provided themselves with rubber sandals made from old car tyres and had advised him to do the same. Finally, someone took pity on him and lent him a spare pair. After the engine had cooled, he climbed back and we all pushed. When the wagon was at last under way, we jumped in. This process was repeated countless times with the result that all we averaged was ten miles an hour. The only other traffic we saw on the road were a procession of camels and two horsemen armed with spears. It was a relief, when at last we drew up outside our first night's rest house. It was just a rough shelter, but to us it seemed like Heaven.

By the following day, our driver had profited from his experiences. Whenever the sand was too thick, he left the road altogether and bumped over open country. As in Sokoto, our faces were coated with dust which clogged our eyebrows and hair and made us and the 'boys' in the back look like circus clowns.

The second night's halt was at the village standing on a huge pimple, composed, so I was told, entirely of dung. Bryan had not wanted to draw attention to our movements, so the village head had had no warning of our arrival. As no European had visited this place for months or perhaps even years, it was hardly surprising that when we reached the rest house we found that it was being used as a stable for the village head's sheep and donkeys. Bryan suggested that I should sit under the shade of a thorn bush while he summoned help from the village. For a full ten minutes, nothing happened. Then suddenly I saw a score of villagers armed with native brooms scrambling up the sandbank towards me. Soon they were inside the rest house and hard at work sweeping. Clouds of dried up dung, ejected from the doorways, were blown into mad eddies by the hot wind. Crouching under my thorn bush with my eyes tightly shut I buried my head in my knees until the dust seemed to have subsided.

That evening, as was his custom, Bryan invited the village head to the rest house for a talk. After the usual lengthy greetings, Bryan asked him how far we were from Lake Chad. 'Ten miles,' said the headman, pointing with his outstretched arm. 'When the moon rises tonight, you will see it shine upon the water.'

His prophecy proved correct. Just as the moon appeared over the horizon, it was reflected along the lake in a thin, shimmering line, which disappeared a few hours later as the moon rose high into the sky.

Although we had kept a watch for the elephants, we saw none. Being sensible animals, they evidently preferred shadier and wetter places to this sandy waste.

Our next halt was at Abadan, a frontier village at the extreme north-east corner of Nigeria. We had had three gruelling days across country which grew more desert like with every mile, so that this tiny, fertile settlement on the Komadugu Yobe River was pure enchantment. There were marabout storks in the bright, green grass which grew on the river banks and rare and beautiful wild geese and duck on its blue water, swimming as unconcernedly as the tame ones do in St James Park. It seemed like a fantasy and I afterwards wondered if I had dreamt it. Even as we journeyed onward the next day, there was a dream-like quality also in the morning mist out of which caravans of camels, mounted by black-veiled Tuaregs, seemed to float from time to time. Then for miles we saw no living thing save rarely a ground squirrel or a monkey and once a gazelle.

When at last we reached the rest house where we were to spend the next night, we decided to open a bottle of the new Nigerian-made orange squash which we had brought with us from Kano. Unfortunately, owing to the heat, fermentation had set in and when Usuman drew out the cork, the contents followed with a bang, leaving the bottle bone dry and Usuman very much astonished.

When at last we returned to Maiduguri, it seemed positively cool by contrast, thanks to a small shower of rain. Instead of returning to Kano by the direct route, we took a much longer but better road via the Plateau. To reach this hilly country, over four thousand feet above sea level, we had to climb by a winding road up a rocky escarpment, where we saw a family of baboons and several grey monkeys. We planned to spend a week at Jos, a pretty, sophisticated hill station and capital of Plateau Province. Unfortunately, I was not able to enjoy the scenery very long, for after two days I was in Jos hospital with amoebic dysentery. In the next room was a Mrs 'Rocks' Wilson, so-called because her husband was Director of Geological Survey. She had the same complaint. Too feeble to communicate in any other way, we amused ourselves with an inter-change of notes, the main topic being food, or rather the lack of it, for we were being fed on nothing but milk drinks. After twelve days of rigorous treatment, we were discharged, shadows of our former selves, but cured.

During my stay in hospital, Bryan had been attached to the Sappers at their headquarters, nine miles from Jos. He had taken a course in blowing up bridges and buildings.

On the day of my discharge, Bryan met me at the hospital with the safari wagon fully-loaded, and we drove direct to Kaduna, capital of the Northern Province and a hundred and seventy miles from Jos.

The Chief Commissioner, Sir Theodore Adams had invited us to stay at Government Lodge later to be re-named 'Government House', and hearing of my illness, asked us to remain a few days until I had gained strength. Immediately after our arrival, we became involved in a reception attended by a number of army officers. Amongst them was a handsome young captain with a heavy moustache nicknamed 'Blood'. He moved in my direction.

'I believe this is your first tour. How do you like the country?' he asked, breezily.

I replied briefly and at the moment honestly, 'Not much'. Poor 'Blood' had made a friendly gesture and felt he had been rebuffed. He went off and told his friends that Mrs Sharwood-Smith was 'formidable'.

However, in these tranquil surroundings I soon began to mend. Early rains had brought fresh greenness to Kaduna and the temperature was no higher than an average summer day in England. Perhaps it was most like the west of England; mild and relaxing. Sir Theodore had come to Kaduna from Malaya three years earlier. Government Lodge was then still new and little had been done to its fifty acres of ground. Sir Theodore and his private secretary were keen landscape gardeners and together they designed a new lay-out with lawns and terraces, shrubberies, two tennis courts and avenues of flame trees. I think quite unique in Nigeria was a paved, formal garden in front of the main entrance, with fountains, standard bougainvillaeas and clipped hibiscus hedges in geometric designs.

Later that afternoon, we had tea on the lawn. Reclining in a wicker chair, munching cucumber sandwiches and sipping tea dispensed by an immaculate steward, I little though that one day this lovely garden would ever in any sense 'belong' to me.

The day after our return to Kano, two ardent Free Frenchmen, whom I shall call Pierre and Francois, called to see Bryan. Frank

Humphries complained that they had been haunting the office most of the time we were away. On this occasion they were in a great state of excitement. They had prepared a manifesto which described Colonel Guilbaud, the French Commander on the Vichy side of our frontier, in the most insulting but flowery French.

'Perhaps Monsieur le Capitaine Sharwood-Smith would be so good as to have copies smuggled over the frontier and placed in every office in Zinder?'

Bryan declined politely but firmly.

'Oh, but perhaps Monsieur le Capitaine does not understand the importance of this document. Perhaps he does not realise what a bad man this Colonel Guilbaud is?'

It was at least an hour before Bryan managed to get rid of them, and emerged from the office, exhausted. Pierre was an ex-government clerk from Dahomey. A little slip of a man, pale with anxiety, his one aim in life was to destroy 'Vichy'. Francois was older and had an aristocratic surname. He was equally fanatical but did occasionally smile, exposing several gold teeth.

Far from understanding the iniquities of this Colonel Guilbaud, Bryan had heard quite the opposite from Langlois who had served under him immediately before his escape from Vichy territory. When Langlois returned, he exchanged occasional letters with his former commander, and not very long after this incident arranged to meet him in a village three miles the other side of the border. It so happened that Bryan and I were on tour at a Nigerian frontier village in the vicinity and Langlois mentioned this to Guilbaud. Nevertheless we had the surprise of our lives when a Vichy French officer in uniform strode into our rest house one afternoon with a message from Colonel Guilbaud, inviting us to a meeting on his side of the border. The opportunity seemed too good to miss. The frontier guards had instructions to admit us, and after a brief enquiry, the bar swung open and we drove through into forbidden territory. Illogically, I expected everything to become suddenly different, more French and more desert-like, but the African at the road side, the dried up trees and parched farmlands were all just the same.

Presently we came to the rest house where the meeting was to take place, an oblong thatched building, mud built. Colonel Guilbaud had his staff officer with him and one or two other officers. After shaking hands warmly with one another, we all sat round a bare wooden table on benches. Guilbaud apologised for the 'Cochonnerie' of the surroundings. He went on to say how deeply he regretted that we were no longer allies. If he were a younger man, he would certainly have accompanied Langlois and Despian to the British side of the frontier to join the Free French.

'I thought deeply over this problem,' he said, 'but I came to the conclusion that it was my duty to stay at my post. Now the Germans have the knife at our throats, but the day will come when we shall rise against them. There is one thing, however, which we cannot understand or forgive, and that is your attack on Oran. Many who were once pro-British changed their minds after that incident.'

He then told us of the film which had been in circulation showing British sailors and airmen firing on the French. Being a Vichy propaganda film it was suspect but nevertheless had an effect. Then Guilbaud stood up, with tears running down his cheeks and said:

'Let us drink to the downfall of the Nazis and may we soon be fighting together to defeat our common enemy!'

We drank this toast in red wine which the French had brought with them. Further expressions of friendship were toasted in the whisky, which was our contribution.

We were much moved by this meeting. Obviously, it was Guilbaud's intention to convey the point of view of many senior Vichy officers and to make it plain that their attitude to us was not as hostile as we had imagined.

Bryan's report on the meeting provoked interested comment in Lagos and in London and the Foreign Office asked for further information. On the other hand, Military Headquarters at Accra felt that such an initiative was uncalled-for and that leave to cross the frontier should first have been obtained.

Back in Kano once more, one of my first tasks was to decipher a 'Top Secret' and 'Most Immediate' announcing the impending arrival of General de Gaulle. Travelling by air and accompanied by General Spears, he was to spend one night in Kano before proceeding to Egypt. Bryan was at once on the telephone to the Resident. It was arranged that the generals should stay at the Residency, but that we should meet them at the airport and, that they should visit us at Gidan Shettima during the evening to discuss Free French affairs.

General de Gaulle was tall and reserved, just as I had expected, but with a wry sense of humour. I conducted him round our house and when we reached the 'baronial hall', where my Bida curtains still hung on the wires across the windows, he remarked gravely, 'Madame, votre maison n'est pas banale.' Afterwards we climbed to the flat roof and had drinks under a star-lit sky. Amongst other things, he asked me my opinion of Langlois and I replied that he was popular and played excellent tennis, but this did not seem quite to satisfy the General and I felt that I had been too frivolous.

My first tour of Nigeria was almost at an end, but before leaving the country, I was asked to help a group of young officers who were being trained to raid deeply into Vichy territory in the event of the Germans overrunning it. My part was to teach them cyphers and to give them hints on survival. This included a number of recipes for simple cooking using the barest equipment and foodstuffs available at any wayside market, and how to pluck a chicken. I also compiled a list and description of edible bush fruits and vegetables.

7 SOUTH AFRICAN INTERLUDE

'No wives,' said the army, 'may on any account return with their husbands to West Africa after going away on leave.'

'But what,' we asked, 'if a wife is employed by the army and is doing valuable work to the War Effort'. We almost dared to add 'irreplaceable?'

'Not, repeat not, under any circumstances,' was the firm answer. Officers with home ties could still take their leave in the United Kingdom, but the dangers of the North Atlantic made long delays in obtaining passages inevitable. Hence, officers were strongly encouraged to take leave in South Africa.

Bryan believed that there might still be some way of wangling me back to Nigeria from South Africa, but that once I set foot in the United Kingdom, there I should stay till the end of the war. So we decided on leave at the Cape. Being July, we should arrive at the height of the South African winter.

I packed sadly. I had so much been looking forward to going home. Far from indispensable as secretary and cypherist, I was at once replaced by two British sergeants. We took the train to Lagos, where we stayed with friends for two weeks, expecting every day to have our sailing orders. At last we had notice to be ready at Apapa Wharf to board *MV Calabar*. The *Calabar* was a miniature passenger liner of only 900 tons. Not built for battling with the high seas, her normal run was between Lagos lagoon and the mangrove swamps of the Niger Delta, passing much of the way through the sultry shelter of the creeks. There were a small number of cabins, each with two bunks, one above the other. The narrow saloon was furnished with scarlet tubular steel chairs and tables and on deck the ship's apparatus left just enough space for the passengers' deck chairs, but no room for exercise.

For two days, we sweltered in Lagos harbour, longing to feel the throb of the engines. Then at last we sailed, through the narrow mouth of the lagoon and out into the Atlantic. Being the middle of the rainy season, the sky was overcast and the sea choppy. The *Calabar* chugged valiantly southward, tossing like a cork. How I hated every grey liquid mile that took me farther from home! There was no ceremonial ducking nor Father Neptune for those like Bryan and me who were 'Crossing the Line' for the first time. With Lord Haw Haw boasting on the air that 'the Germans would get the *Calabar* this time' there was no inclination for frivolity. Fortunately, it was an idle threat. The packs of Nazi U Boats in the South Atlantic found bigger and more interesting fish than the little *Calabar*.

After passing, one night, the lights of the Portuguese island of São Thomé, the days passed, oh so slowly, until ten days later we sighted land once more, near Walfish Bay. Three days later through pouring rain we had our first view of the Table Mountain. It was heavily blanketed with cloud. We anchored some distance from land and presently were met by a launch. Three port officials climbed on board in dripping oilskins with the news that no berth would be available in Cape Town docks till the next day. Then came the announcement on the ship's loud speakers. 'Any passengers wishing to go ashore tonight may take the launch on its return journey with their hand-baggage only.' Bryan and I hastened to volunteer, but we need not have hurried for we were the only passengers to do so. There was a heavy swell and as we faltered down the lower rungs of the rope ladder, we found that the launch was dropping a giddy six feet into the trough of each wave. The remaining passengers leaned over the rail and gazed at us with some amusement. Nervously, we chose our moment and stepped in, then waved back triumphantly as we sped thankfully towards the shore.

PART TWO

8 THE RAINS FAIL IN SOKOTO, EMERGENCY MEASURES

All too soon, Bryan's short leave came to an end and we were once more waving 'Goodbye' as he left for Nigeria. Our separation this time was to last a whole year. So there I was, 6,000 miles from home expecting a baby, though by no means the only lonely wife in South Africa. Apart from the local ones, there must have been thousands of British women with their children in the Cape, evacuated from war zones in the Mediterranean area and the Far East. I found rooms with one, a doctor's wife from Hong Kong. I also found myself a job, connected with the local security organisation, and continued working until shortly before Michael to my great joy was born seven months later.

Bryan meanwhile, on his return to Nigeria, continued his service with the Nigeria Regiment, but was based on Lagos instead of Kano, much to his disappointment. After nine months, the war moved out of the African continent so there was no further need of a transfrontier intelligence organisation. He was therefore released from the army and returned to the administrative services. Unfortunately, while there he developed a more than usually severe attack of asthma, a complaint which was apt to afflict him in the rains when the millet was in pollen. He wrote to me telling me of the asthma and sounding ill and depressed but also saying that he had permission for me to join him. At any other time, this last news would have filled me with delight, but now there was Michael and he was four months old. To take him with me to Nigeria was not then possible. In the first place, the Nigerian government did not normally permit officers to have their children with them. The health risks were considered too great. Sokoto was one of the hottest provinces in the North with a poor record for health as far as Europeans were concerned. So I was faced with the agonising decision of whether to stay in the Cape with Michael or whether to find a reliable nurse to look after him there while I returned to my sick husband in Nigeria. As Bryan and I had

63

already been separated for practically a year, this seemed the wisest course in the interests of all three of us. I hoped that I should be able to return to Michael after not more than six months absence.

It so happened that, while I was alone in the Cape, I had made friends with another Nigerian DO and his wife, Gwilym and Ursula Jones. They were on leave from the Eastern Provinces. Gwilym and Ursula were exceptionally helpful to me at the time of Michael's birth, their own first child, Jocelyn having been born only a few weeks before. Ursula wanted to find a nanny to look after her baby while she returned for a short time to Nigeria with Gwilym, so we made enquiries and eventually it was they who found an excellent English trained children's nurse prepared to take both our children. Another good friend agreed to be Michael's godmother and guardian and she and the nurse wrote regularly during my absence, giving news of Michael's progress.

So I sailed for Nigeria, with a sad and heavy heart. Bryan met me at Gusau, the nearest railway station to Sokoto, for this was where by this time he had been posted. The move had proved beneficial since his asthma subsided and he seemed in reasonable health.

Instead of driving directly to Sokoto, 140 miles away and settling into our new home, we had to go straight away on tour to the northern frontier where the cattle thieves from French territory had been giving trouble. We spent the night in an empty African house in the middle of Gusau town and set out before dawn the next morning by van. The Sardauna came with us as the Sultan's representative. After two days driving, the motor road petered out into a narrow track. The district head met us at this point with horses for the rest of the journey. Mine was a temperamental grey which had evidently been trained for ceremonial purposes. He had a showy way of standing on his hind legs and waving the front ones in the air. A sharp kick in the ribs set him off at a smart canter but, whenever stony ground caused the procession to slow down, the dancing started again. Sometimes he moved sideways, like a crab, and bucked. My muscles were in no state for this kind of riding and, after five or six miles, I gave up and changed horses with one of the policemen who were accompanying us. If the grey had objected to my modest weight, he was even more vehement about the burly policeman, who was soon off and rolling in the dust.

At last we arrived at our destination, the town of Sabon Birni. Although it was only October, the dry season was unusually well advanced and the people looked drab and listless. As we passed through the outskirts of the town, we saw the charred remains of the rest house which had just been accidentally burnt down. Instead, the Court House had been put at our disposal. Its grandiose title belied it, for it was just a small, bare mud-built hall in the middle of the town. We had scarcely unpacked, when the district head arrived with the news that one of the local farmers had been shot dead on the Nigerian side of the border by (African) French mounted police. It appeared that he had been on a trip into French territory when he had been spotted by a police patrol and chased back into Nigeria. A friend of the murdered farmer, who had been with him at the time, had come with the district head to give an eye witness account of the incident. He said, 'When I saw the French policeman was going to shoot, I called out, "We are home, we are home!" but he took no notice and fired.'

Bryan at once despatched a horseman to alert a troop of mounted levies who were encamped about thirty miles away. These irregulars had been recruited, as a wartime measure, from the most spirited younger men of the Emir's households. Their purpose was to protect the frontier against possible incursions of this nature. The levies were a tough, hard-riding lot with a reputation for loose living and drinking. However, as soon as our appeal for help reached the British subaltern in command, they set out and, riding through the night, caught up with us by breakfast.

The idea was to leave me alone at the Court House in Sabon Birni while the rest of the party rode to the scene of the crime. But the thought of spending a solitary day in that stuffy little hall did not appeal to me so I persuaded Bryan to let me go with him and we all rode off together. By this time, I was in better trim, which was just as well, for the track was exceedingly rough and we rode through the heat of the day. When we arrived we were able to identify the spot by a pool of dried blood. We were only half a mile from the frontier and in full view of a village in French territory. Bryan made further enquiries of the local people. The levies then fired a burst of tommy gun fire into the air as a warning to the Vichy authorities not to repeat the crime and we returned to Sabon Birni.

A week later, we were at last at Sokoto and I had unpacked my tin trunks and hung up my clothes in the wardrobe of the SDO's house. The Resident was an ex-naval officer named Commander Carrow. A tall man with a large head, rugged features and deep-set eyes, he displayed a truly awful wrath towards any who failed to reach his high standards of efficiency. But he was a sociable man. The deep-set eyes could twinkle and the lion-like head be thrust back with gales of laughter. The people of Sokoto admired and respected him. Mrs Carrow was, by contrast, petite and dainty. She liked long necklaces and jangly bangles. Before her marriage she had been an education officer in Northern Nigeria and, at this time, she was acting DO Finance. Owing to the war, there was still an acute shortage of younger male administrative officers, despite which she was, I think, the only woman ever to hold such an appointment in the North.

Before long, I too was found occupation, though mine was unofficial. My first task was to help combat a serious shortage of corn; for the drought which had made Sabon Birni so drab and lifeless had cast its blight over much of the province.

Two varieties of corn were grown by Sokoto farmers, bulrush millet and guinea corn, and these were the staple foods. In a good year, both kinds were sown after the first heavy downpour, which usually took place in early May. As the young shoots sprang up, they needed further rain about every seven to ten days to keep them healthy. By June, the quicker growing bulrush millet would be waist high. Daily soakings throughout July would cause even faster and more robust growth and by August this millet would be up to ten feet high with a thick stalk and a spike at the top eighteen inches tall, wreathed in cobwebby strands of pollen. Under this cover, the seeds grew and swelled and by late August, the rain would have washed off the pollen and the millet would be ripe and ready for harvesting.

The slower growing guinea corn, on the other hand, did not mature until November. Unlike the earlier variety, its seeds grew in wavy fronds, like a giant grass, and it reached twelve to fifteen feet, so high as to touch the telegraph wires in places. Guinea corn stalks were as thick and strong as bamboo and, after the harvest, they were stacked in stooks for use later as fences, roofs and beds.

But this year had not followed the normal pattern. The rains had started well but, towards the end of May, they ceased. Day after day passed with clear skies, while anxious farmers watched the young corn droop and wither. By the time that the weather changed, most of it was dead. The result was an almost complete failure of the bulrush millet. The corn sellers in the market were swift to take advantage of the threatened hunger. They hoarded as much grain from the previous harvest as they could lay hands on and proceeded to sell it, a little at a time, at exorbitant prices.

The shortage was most acute in Sokoto city itself where there was a large non-farming population of traders and clerical workers.

Fortunately, there were areas in the south of the province where the rains had been fairly normal. So, to fight the black market and provide a rationing system, the Native Administration bought corn in these more plentiful areas. There were no all season motor roads linking them with Sokoto, so camels and donkeys had to be used as a means of transport. Every available animal was commandeered and, after two or three weeks, the NA had accumulated enough corn to start supplying the hospital, the schools and prison and to provide a small ration for every government employee and his family. The rest was sold to the public in the market at the rate of one calabash-full per person. This was of a standard size and contained about two and a quarter pounds of corn. But some greedy market women were not to be lightly deprived of their profit and they managed to give short measure by quick, sly movements with the calabash. After consultation with the Sultan, however, a heavier wooden measure, which could not be manipulated, was made compulsory. But it was a constant battle of wits and police were on duty all day at the specially barricaded corn-stalls to prevent fighting, cheating and queue jumping.

My job was to calculate the transport cost per measure for each purchasing centre and the amount due to each camel and donkey owner, averaging out to a standard charge. I was then asked to make lists of those entitled to rations and to help our only ADO to weigh out the corn for the office staff and messengers.

As time passed, the guinea corn, which had largely survived the drought, began to ripen. The would-be profiteers were forced to place hoarded corn on the market and the price dropped to nearly normal. The rationing tactics had succeeded.

I was not left long in idleness to brood over my separation from my little boy, before another task was found for me. This was the re-organisation of the Native Administration Central Office, a spacious, brick building in the middle of the city. The mallams who ran it had had no office training and only one of them could speak English. Bryan wanted me to introduce the same simple filing and card index system which we had used at Gidan Shettima during the Research Office days at Kano. Of course, at other times, this would have been an ADO's task, but, with the exception of our one young man, who was fully occupied elsewhere, they were all in the forces.

Sometimes, in the evenings, I used to visit the Girls' Training Centre, where I had friends amongst the four British women who formed the teaching staff. This was a college for girls who had passed through the local elementary school and wished to take up teaching. They were given a general education with emphasis on domestic subjects and handicrafts. The Centre was protected by a wall nine feet high from would-be Romeos, for the girls were in their teens and at their most attractive. In fact, had they not been furthering their education, they would all have been married. The first headmistress was a Miss Booker, a lady of notoriously firm character. It was she who insisted on the wall. In pre-war days, one of the DO's had been rash enough to take a visiting French administrateur unannounced to see the college, which was then something of a show piece. But Miss Booker, evidently fearing for her pupils' virtue, had refused the Frenchmen entry. 'Mon Dieu!' breathed the poor man on leaving the Centre, 'Mais, c'est une veritable gorgonne!'

A few years later a sports meeting was held at Sokoto Boys' Middle School, where, for the first time, one of the youths cleared nine feet at the pole vault. Someone amongst the spectators was heard to exclaim triumphantly, 'There goes the Booker wall!'

To teach the pupils domestic science, the school had built an imaginative model compound inside the college grounds. This followed the same pattern as the pupils' own homes, though it was neater and better furnished and had one or two European touches, such as bright check curtains on the windows. There were the usual huts, a large one for the master of the house, smaller ones for the wives, a kitchen hut, corn stores and so on. Once, when I came to the school, there was great excitement because one of the married pupils had produced a baby. A European type of cot with a mosquito net had been provided for the infant in one of the huts of the model home and there it was, all tucked up, in a nightdress and nappies. 'We keep the baby in its cot as much as possible,' a European teacher told me. 'It is so bad for them to share their mother's beds and risk suffocation. We are also trying to teach the girls that it is wrong to carry babies on their backs. It could so easily cause a curvature of the spine.' I could not help wondering how it was that so many Africans had normal backs since all of them must have been carried in this way in infancy. However, the child did not have to endure such spartan treatment all the time, because whenever the staff were away, the temptation to give the baby pick-a-back rides was too much for the girls.

One day, when Sardauna was having tea with us, he told us that his wife had given birth to a little girl. We congratulated him and felt pleased that he had told us this news, for it was not the custom in Muslim circles to discuss wives and children except with the most intimate of friends.

I had just finished making a matinee jacket for Michael and had posted it to South Africa. So I decided to cut out and make a similar one for Sardauna's daughter, embroidering it to make it pretty enough for a little girl. In due course, the baby's mother wrote to thank me in neat handwriting and delightful English. She began by using my Christian name and, after thanks and the usual greetings, she went on to say that she was sure that our husbands would one day be great leaders. At the time, this did not seem at all likely for Bryan had no ambitions and Sardauna's controversial nature made him at times a difficult member of the Sultan's Council.

At last came the time for us to return to South Africa and for Bryan to see his son for the first time. Michael had grown into a sturdy little boy and had just started walking. He had rosy cheeks, a mop of blond hair and cornflower blue eyes with which he regarded us with some astonishment. His nurse had certainly taken good care of him and perhaps, naturally, she did not show any great keeness to hand him over. We began to get to know him gently, by taking him out for walks and returning him to the nurse.

Meanwhile, we were searching high and low for a furnished flat, for the Cape still seethed with war evacuees and vacant ones were rare. In the end, by luck, we found one on the lower slopes of Table Mountain in a suburb called Tamboers Kloof. We then equipped it with the baby paraphernalia; a cot, play pen and push chair and, most important, the latest book on child care. Then came the exciting moment when we took Michael 'home'.

It was summer in South Africa, a gentle, balmy heat compared with Nigeria; a time for country walks and picnics. The only push chair we had been able to find was a seat on wheels at the end of a broomstick, rather like an ambulatory shopping basket. It had to be carefully steered over rough ground for it had no springs, but at least it was easily lifted into buses for expeditions which were beyond walking distance. A favourite one was over a mountain pass called Kloof Nek and down to Camps Bay, a rocky cove where the blue sea of the South Atlantic lapped a shore of dazzling white sand.

Pushing our child up the steep slopes at the foot of Table Mountain, every time we went shopping, was rather exhausting, but at least we were rewarded for our efforts by the glorious view we had from every window, across Table Bay. Here the big ships moved silently in and out, or lay at anchor. Across the water were the mountains of the mainland, their summits just showing over wreaths of feathery clouds.

9 TO MINNA WITH MICHAEL

Bryan's leave lasted a meagre eight weeks but for me the parting was less painful than the last one had been since it was for a shorter time and now I had Michael with me. We waved 'Goodbye' at Cape Town dock gates and then took the bus to Green Point and waved again as his ship steamed past on its way out to sea. When Michael and I reached our flat in Tamboers Kloof, it seemed dreadfully quiet and empty.

Meanwhile, Bryan was on his way to Minna, where he had been appointed substantive Resident, not 'acting' as before. The plan was that I should join him there six months later, bringing Michael with me. The Nigerian government was by this time more amenable to requests by parents to have their children with them. Moreover, we were not so worried about the health risks. Minna, though enervating, was not as hot as Sokoto nor so plagued with flies. Also, as Resident, Bryan was now in control and no longer liable to be transferred at short notice from one part of the Province to another, nor to be sent off without warning on tour. We hoped to have Michael out for a short tour and then return with him to England. We were now in the year 1944 and the war appeared at last to be drawing to a close.

Bryan had a number of ideas about making parts of the Residency more suitable for a child. Extra guest accommodation had already been built in the form of a chalet in the garden with a verandah which could make a pleasant and shady place for Michael to play in when otherwise not wanted.

A few weeks after Bryan left us, Michael developed a severe and prolonged attack of glandular fever and I was not able to put our names down at the shipping agents' until he had properly recovered. By the time that the passages were booked, I had been in South Africa a further nine months and Michael was almost two years old. Our ship was an obsolete vessel which had once belonged to Elder Dempster's fleet, and was overdue to be

71

scrapped. But sinkings by the enemy had been so heavy that it was decided instead to convert her into a troop ship. The operation had been slow and, in the end, the Admiral had lost patience and had ordered that the ship must be ready by a definite date. Accordingly, this was the day we sailed. But the ship's blackout arrangements were only half-finished and no-one had thought fit to place a notice over the entrance to the lavatories to say whether they were for men or women. Nor had they any outside doors. There were no baths nor hot water for washing. As the ship's officers showed no willingness to carry out improvements, the passengers took matters into their own hands. Counterpanes were pinned across the toilet doors, appropriate labels for Ladies and Gentlemen were pinned over them and, with the co-operation of some helpful Goanese stewards, hipbaths and hot water were brought up from some hidden source below. At least it was now possible to bath the children, for there were two others besides Michael. We were just beginning to feel some satisfaction at the way we had organised ourselves when an ominous silence fell. The engines had failed. Throughout the night we drifted helplessly, a sitting duck for any German U boat that chanced our way. Next day tugs reached us from Cape Town to tow us back to port. Ropes were tossed several times in our direction but, characteristically, each time the ship's crew failed to catch them. Eventually, the tug master gave up and returned to port. The ship's engineers then did some sober thinking, with the result that the engines started up again and we steamed back to Cape Town.

So there I was, back in the Cape, but with a baby and without any money. I had closed my account with the Standard Bank before leaving and had only enough cash to last the voyage. The other mother on board was in the same predicament, so we asked to be allowed to stay there while the repairs were carried out. All the rest of the passengers went to hotels. Ten days later, they rejoined us and we sailed north once more.

Michael and I were in a single cabin into which six berths had been ingeniously squeezed. They were arranged in tiers of three on each side. The occupants were four women and two small children. The portholes were hermetically sealed at night as a 'black-out' precaution, so our cabin became hot and airless as we sailed into the tropics. One of the passengers was an ample blonde who came in late each night after spending the evening in the Captain's cabin. Her first act was to switch on the lights, light a cigarette and, despite my complaints, tell us in a loud voice what

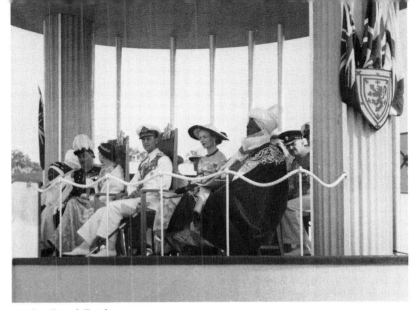

At the Royal Durbar
Front row: Sir Abubaker, Sultan of Sokoto, Bryan, HM the Queen,
HRH the Duke of Edinburgh, JSS, Sir Ahmadu Bello, Sardauna of
Sokoto

A festive day for Kano. The Emir receives the honour of knighthood
from Bryan (for the Queen)

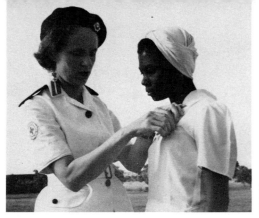

A young member of the
Red Cross receives her
badge

Above:
At the Police Sports, JSS
presents the cup

A Sokoto snake charmer
shows his tricks

Garden party at Kaduna for members of the House of Assembly.
Angela hands round the cakes

The Capital School of Kaduna

Kano City

the captain had said. Both babies woke and watched her spell-bound. In desperation, I took to dragging two mattresses onto the deck at night, where it was not exactly quiet but at least it was cool and fresh.

After a fortnight, we arrived safely and thankfully at Lagos. Rex and Dorothy Niven, who were then stationed at Lagos, gave us shelter at their home in the residential suburb of Ikoyi, until we were able to catch the North bound train. One afternoon our host took Michael and me to Victoria beach. A white child, even in Lagos, was still a novelty and people on the beach turned and stared at him. Michael was quite unconcerned though rather hot. On the train he suffered still more and came out all over in 'prickly heat', a tropical rash which we all had from time to time though not to this extent. Poor Michael looked like a bad case of measles.

It was a relief to arrive at the familiar station of Minna. As usual, in the middle of the afternoon, a brassy sun blazed down and only the faintest of sultry breezes stirred the leaves of the mango trees which gave some shade to the platform, but we cooled down quickly enough when we reached the Residency.

Michael soon settled into the new routine and was a great favourite with the domestic staff and the messengers. They were highly amused when, like Daddy, he gave orders. For this they nicknamed him 'Captain Michael'. We particularly asked them not to speak to him in pidgin English, so they taught him Hausa in which he was soon more fluent than in English. When I was away in Kaduna for a minor operation, even Bryan unconsciously dropped into the habit of talking to Michael in Hausa. This was not surprising for we were all bilingual in those days, and he did find it so much easier to understand.

The only other white children were the son and daughter of the superintendent of the Hausa School for missionaries. We felt very sorry for these children who were ill for several weeks after we arrived. No sooner had they recovered from dysentery than they were in bed again with malaria, after which they came out in tropical boils. I expect that they had stayed far too long in a climate as enervating as Minna, but the Missions could not afford to send their staff and families on leave more than once every three years. When at last the children were well, we invited the whole family to tea at the Residency. The grown-ups had tea sedately on the terrace while the children played in the garden. Rather to our surprise, we discovered that our children were talking to one another in Hausa. As Bryan and I wanted Michael to learn to speak the language we did not mind, but the Missionary parents were rather concerned, perhaps afraid that their children might be growing up unable to speak proper English.

When Christmas came, we decided to give a children's party, inviting the sons and daughters of such local Nigerian notables as the station master, the postmaster and the senior Government clerks with their parents. This idea was quite new to the Africans in Minna and they were perplexed and even a little affronted. However, after a little coaxing, they agreed to lend themselves to this curious experiment. We borrowed trestle tables for the garden and loaded them with cakes, jellies and crackers. After tea there were games and races for the children. One or two parents became rather distressed when their children failed to win. However, we tried to explain to them that it was all just a game and when at last they all went home, we felt sure that the experiment had been a success.

As Resident, Bryan had to tour the four divisions of which Niger Province was composed. As all but one of these divisions were cooler than Minna, Michael and I usually went with him.

Abuja, ninety miles in the hills to the south east was a favourite and refreshing haunt. After three hours drive on a winding road, we climbed steeply to the crest of the hill, on which stood the district officer's bungalow and the rest house.

A Native Administration policeman saluted and directed us to the rest house. It was a shady, rambling building with an overhanging thatched roof. Looking down the hill from the garden, we could see Abuja town below, clusters of round huts over which wood smoke hovered lazily.

The country people were pagan Gwaris, like those living round Minna, but the Emir and many of the townfolk were Hausa. It seemed that his ancestors had once been kings of Zaria, one of the original Hausa states, a hundred miles to the north. Early in the nineteenth century, they had been driven out by Shehu dan Fodio's Fulani army, who had surprised them on the day of the great Salla, right in the middle of their prayers. The terrified Zaria people were confused and scattered but the Emir managed to escape with three thousand followers. He fled south and, after many wanderings, settled at Abuja. Here, he and his successors resisted the Fulani enemy until British occupation brought tribal fightings to and end. Abuja people still assembled inside the city walls to celebrate the festivals, not outside as was the normal custom. The Emir led his people in prayer facing east, but his bodyguard of archers kept watch to the west in remembrance of the day of disaster.

Old enmities had long since been forgotten. But, like other visitors, we were shown the place where every male Fulani that fell into Abuja hands was once executed. At this spot, known as 'Maiyanka' which meant 'Slaughter slab' a river drops vertically from a cliff to boulders a hundred feet below. The custom was first to cut off the victim's right hand and to send it to the Emir as proof that the execution had taken place. The prisoner was then hurled into the foaming waters.

The Emir told us this story as we walked round the city that evening. A slim, young man with a deep voice, he spoke English fluently. Like Sardauna, he had been educated at Katsina College.

While in the town, we called at the Primary School, where one of the teachers was a girl named Tani, who had just left Sokoto Girls' Training Centre. She was an attractive and high spirited young woman, aged about eighteen. Tani was delighted to see us and showed us some of her pupils' drawings.

Next we called to see the dispensary, a simple white-washed building which, judging by the smell, had only just been scrubbed with carbolic. The attendant was immaculately dressed in a white scull cap and gown. Locally, he was known as the 'Likita', the Hausa version of the word 'Doctor'. As the Medical Officer lived in Minna and was only occasionally able to tour Abuja, it was the dispensary attendant's job to care for the town's sick most of the time. He was trained to give first aid and to administer medicines for all the more usual complaints such as coughs, fever, dysentery and worm conditions. He had large jars of stock mixtures, each carefully numbered and labelled and he painstakingly recorded the attendances of his patients and their complaints. Not long before our visit, a maternity extension had been added to the dispensary, presided over by a qualified African midwife. It was equipped with couches for two patients. The midwife told us that she was having some difficulty in persuading mothers to avail themselves of her services, instead of having their babies delivered in the old fashioned way, squatting on a birth stool in a corner of the compound, attended by one of the grannies.

The country surrounding Abuja was undulating woodland out of which, to the south east, a great, basalt rock a thousand feet high jutted upward like a black molar tooth. This was called the Zuma rock and it was said to be haunted. The story was that a community of invisible people lived in a thickly wooded dell at the foot of the rock and protected it from strangers. The people from the next village were too frightened to intrude, but they brought the invisible people gifts from time to time and as these always disappeared, they assumed that they had been accepted. It was even said that the guardians of the rock made animal and human sacrifices to appease the spirits. The Emir himself in bygone days had made an annual contribution of a black ox, a black she-goat and a black dog.

A few years earlier, before the Emir had succeeded his father, he determined to get to the bottom of these tales. He set out for the mysterious village with the district officer and two junior NA officials. When they reached the nearby hamlet to enquire the way, the people were appalled by such audacity and warned them that the priest would not speak to them and they were most unlikely to emerge alive. When finally they realised that the investigators would not be deterred, they showed them the way but refused to accompany them. At last the party reached its destination only to find that the priest and people were visible, normally dressed and that they even spoke Hausa. They welcomed their unexpected guests hospitably and showed them the place where animal sacrifices were made. But they denied all knowledge of human sacrifices, except as a legend of olden times. However, all these years the story had served its purpose, which was to frighten away foreigners, particularly their enemies the Fulani.

The Emir of Abuja took a great interest in Michael and, a few years later, when on a visit to England, travelled from London to Warwick especially to see him at his preparatory school. It was a red letter day for the whole school as well as for Michael when this charming but modest man arrived in his full chiefly dress of turban, kaftan and gown.

Our next tour was to our old home of Kontagora, where the Emir was pleased to note, amid many chuckles, that my Hausa had improved. The day after we arrived was the great Muslim festival, the *Salla*. The European guests watched the spectacle from a row of seats placed a little distance from the prayer ground outside the city walls and, as at Sokoto, it was the Emir's custom to greet them after the rites with the words '*Barka da Salla!*' meaning 'Blessings on the Salla', the local equivalent of 'Happy Christmas'. Unfortunately, as he drew near, with his servant rotating the ceremonial umbrella overhead, Michael was seized with fright and screamed.

From Kontagora, we went on to Zuru, an old garrison town not far from the Sokoto border. This was the land of the 'Daks'

(Dakakerri) a tribe of war-like pagans of outstanding physique. The men wore leather loin cloths and the women two bunches of leaves which hung, fore and aft, below the waist. We saw several processions in single file, by the road side carrying heavy loads to the market on their heads. Michael liked Zuru and was not at all worried by the bats which swooped to and fro inside the rest house. On the other hand, he was not quite so happy about the camel which was brought to the rest house compound especially to amuse him. The beast would have been all right if it had remained standing, but its owner, wanting to show off its tricks, told it to lie down. It collapsed itself, joint by joint, and Michael was convinced that it had come to pieces.

We tried a succession of remedies for Michael's prickly heat, including an old local cure made from an infusion of tamarind pods. Although this helped a little, the rash never quite left him. The hot and humid climate of Niger Province was against us and so was his restless energy. His favourite day time sport in Minna was bowling an empty 44-gallon petrol drum round the garden.

One of the walks he enjoyed most was 'to see the cows being milked'. They lived at a small Fulani encampment about half a mile away, tended by a herdsman and his wives and children. The camp consisted of a collection of 'beehive' huts, made of grass thatching on a framework of corn stalks. During the day, the sons drove the cattle out to graze and at evening time, brought them back and tethered them in an enclosure. This was firmly fenced with branches of thorn bush to protect the animals from hyenas and leopards.

Fulani cows had a trick of withholding their milk unless they believed they were suckling their young. So the herdsmen used to allow a calf to suck for a while. He then artfully withdrew it and continued milking by hand into a pail.

The cattle were longer in the leg than the European variety, with heavier, angular bones and fleshy humps on their backs. Huge, curved horns jutted out of their heads like great ivory, hay-forks. When a cow lowered her head, she was a fearsome sight, especially when seen from the front. Michael wisely kept his distance, but was not really afraid. The Fulani were delighted to see the little white boy. They at once started teaching him their language. 'Have you had a good day?', 'Been to the market?', 'Have a good night', etc. Bryan spoke Fulani, which was unusual in a European, and used to exchange jokes with the herdsmen and make his wife and children giggle.

The herd was the source of the Residency milk. We paid the herdsman a regular wage and allowed him grazing rights. In return, he supplied us with unwatered milk. Fulani were notorious for adulterating milk to the extent that many Europeans preferred to use tinned milk. However, we had an instrument for detecting water in milk and the Fulani knew this. So the arrangement worked well.

After a year in Minna, Michael and I left by sea for England. We sailed on 4 March 1945 and arrived on 5 April, a journey of four and a half weeks instead of the normal twelve days. Though the end of the war in Europe was drawing close, we were warned to have our life belts with us all the time, even at meals. We travelled all the way by convoy and the male passengers took turns to watch for German submarines. I was fully occupied keeping an eye on my energetic child. The sides of the decks were open except for an arm railing and were very dangerous for a toddler. He all but slipped overboard many times. Children were not allowed in the saloons lest they disturb the passengers, so I was obliged to keep Michael in the cabin or on deck all the time. If it rained we sought refuge in the bar, which for some strange reason was not banned to children, though, as Michael was invariably attracted to the noisiest table, I did not resort to it too often. Ours was the flag-ship of the convoy. The Commodore was English, but a Buddhist and wore a black beret most of the time. He took a fancy to Michael and one day led him up to the bridge and showed him his charts and other nautical apparatus.

Once again, we were lucky to escape the attentions of the enemy. Just the same, when we finally sighted the English coast, we were so relieved that one of the passengers produced a penny whistle and played 'There'll always be an England' and we all felt rather emotional. Our first view was of Portland Bill and we naturally expected to dock at Portsmouth. However, after thirty hours at anchor, much to our disappointment, we sailed to Southend. As we passed through the 'Downs' we had to thread our way through the procession of ships and landing-craft which were crossing the Channel to supply the allied armies in France. When we reached the Thames Estuary, it was a sorry sight. There were hundreds of wrecked ships on either side, their masts sticking out of the water at rakish angles. Where ships were completely submerged, their position was marked by bell-buoys, which tolled a mournful lament in the morning breeze. Again, we waited for a day and a half, hoping to land, only to be told that

Southend had no facilities for receiving passengers. So we sailed for the open sea again and we docked two days later at Hull. The following morning, Michael and I were seated, miraculously, so it seemed, in an express train, which tore through the fields of England on its way to London.

There was so much to amaze a three-year-old on his first trip to Britain. First there was the speed of the train, for in those days the Nigerian ones seldom chugged along faster than twenty five miles an hour. Then there were the snowflakes which beat upon the carriage window, for though it was early April, it was bitterly cold. When I told him that the squat, short horned creatures he could see grazing in the meadows were cows, he flatly refused to believe me, they were so different from the stately hump-backed cattle at Minna.

On reaching London, we were pushed and jostled by the crowds and had to stand in a long queue for a taxi. However, we finally completed the last lap of our journey and reached Leamington where my parents were eagerly awaiting us. They were delighted with their first view of their grandson, though they thought him rather pale. But the sight of me appalled them for I was six years older, I had lost a stone in weight and the new drug mepacrin, which I had been taking to ward off malaria, had turned me yellow. To cap it all, another baby was on the way.

However, it was lovely to be home at last. Even the buttercups in the garden, foul weeds to my father, were a joy to me. And oh, what bliss to drink tea with fresh milk, for in Nigeria it always had to be boiled.

Two months later, the war with Germany ended amid much jubilation. But those who hoped for an early end to food rationing were disappointed. Supplies seemed to be smaller than ever. The weekly adult ration was four ounces of meat, two ounces of butter and one egg and there was a daily ration of a quarter of a pint of milk. Tinned and certain other foods were obtained through a complicated system of points and though meat pies, sausages and fish were unrationed, we had to wait for them in long and tedious queues. Despite this, the quality of food was much higher than in Nigeria. Also, expectant mothers and children under five were allowed certain extras. So Michael and I were not hungry and we steadily improved in health.

Nevertheless, as Michael's skin had suffered from the climate of Minna, to the extent that it took six weeks of specialist treatment to put it right, I did not think that I ought to take him back with me when the time came for me to return, though I hated the idea of leaving him again. However, there was no need to dwell on that gloomy thought, for the new baby was not due for another six months and I did not intend to return to Nigeria until he was at least eight months old. My mother found us a furnished house in Leamington and shortly after we had settled in, Bryan arrived home for leave. He stayed with us until a few days after the new baby Geoffrey was born, then went back to Minna. I planned to join him only for the middle six of his eighteen months' tour.

10 ALL THE FAMILY TO SOKOTO

Of course, I missed my little boys terribly when I arrived back in Minna and our Nigerian friends could not imagine why I had left them behind. I tried to explain that their climate was not good for white children, but they did not seem to understand. As some sort of compensation, we acquired two dogs, Gogo, an English cocker spaniel and a fox terrier of mixed African and European parentage named Poppy.

Each morning, before breakfast, I used to exercise the dogs on the airfield which was about half a mile from the Residency. Quite often, they startled a gazelle which used to graze there. The buck escaped with swift, graceful leaps into the air, while the dogs tore after her, panting. Gogo's long ears streaming behind him like banners.

Sometimes, in the evenings, we used to bundle dogs and guns into the car and drive a short distance along the road to Zungeru. Then we would leave the car by the roadside and trudge into the bush, hoping to shoot a wild guinea fowl or two for the pot. One day, we had walked about a mile when we came to a dried up water course in which grew dwarf palm trees and creepers. Poppy's African instincts warned her that this dark place was dangerous and she wisely kept out. Gogo, the heedless, trotted straight in. We called and called, but to no avail. Presently, a much larger, dun-coloured creature emerged lazily from the far end of the thicket. A long tail with a dark tuft at the end hung limply between his hind legs. The animal paused on a rock and half turned its head in our direction. Then it sprang softly onto the next rock and loped off. Gogo had 'put up' a young lion. For a moment, we feared for his life but he joined us a few minutes later, wagging his feathery tail furiously.

As Michael and Geoffrey were too young to read letters, we sent them a weekly bulletin in the form of pictures. Mine were news items, in which Poppy and Gogo often figured. Bryan drew cartoons of imaginary characters called Horace and Horatia Hartebeest and their friends. It made us feel in touch.

When Bryan had completed another tour of Minna, during which, as before, I joined him just for the middle six months, he was moved to Sokoto. Although we were sorry to say good-bye to our good friends in Niger Province, we were thrilled to be returning to Sokoto. The Residency was an old and gloomy bungalow, but a new one, three times the size was planned and work soon began. This was to be on one floor only also, for Sokoto 'station' was founded on sand and would not take the weight of a two storyed building. The site was on the crest of a stony slope which faced Sokoto's beautiful gardens. It was exciting, watching this large new house taking shape and laying out its grounds. We decided to have three terraces built on the eroded slope. The top two we had planted with flower beds and lawns and the bottom one we turned into an orchard. The trees and shrubs included oranges, grapefruit, guavas and cape goose-berries. As fruit trees are delicate in a climate as dry and windy as Sokoto, we asked the advice of Mr Vigo, an agricultural officer who specialised in fruit growing. He had a flourishing orchard at Gusau where he grew the finest and sweetest oranges I ever tasted in Nigeria. They were dark green on the outside and almost red in their juicy insides. Mr Vigo was a cultured West Indian whom Africans paradoxically described as the 'Baturen Gona', literally the 'white man of the farm'. He and Dr Franklin, the Gusau Medical Officer, who was a Yoruba, belonged to the European community of Gusau and were popular members of its Club.

As the new Residency grew, we pondered the possibility of bringing the children out the next tour. Sokoto could certainly be hotter than Minna but it was drier, so there was no risk of the prickly heat, which had plagued Michael before. Also, the new house would be more spacious and comfortable than any of our previous homes. But another problem, more serious than the climate, was the prevalence of dysentery. This affected both Africans and Europeans but whereas the Africans had some inborn resistance to the disease, the Europeans had none and many had been invalided from Sokoto because of it. The disease was carried by flies which swarmed everywhere. Fortunately, a sensational new insecticide had just appeared on the market, the now familiar DDT. The medical officer had the inside walls of all the houses in Sokoto station, including the new Residency, sprayed, as an experiment. The result was a great success. The treated houses remained totally free of flies for months.

These small improvements were, however, as nothing compared with developments elsewhere in the country.

Up to the time of the Second World War, Nigeria had had to pay her way on a meagre revenue of £8 million. So much was absorbed by Lagos and the other important centres for public buildings, docks, hospitals etc, that there was little left for remoter places such as Sokoto. The administrative officers and their colleagues in the various departments needed all the resourcefulness and ingenuity they could muster to make any progress at all. At this time, the oil which later brought wealth to Nigeria, had not been discovered.

In 1940, in the darkest period of the war, Britain suddenly awoke to her colonies' need for capital and the Colonial Development and Welfare Act was passed. The effect of this was not felt in Nigeria until 1945, when she received a grant of £23 million of the British tax-payers' money for a ten-year capital development plan. The country was by this time richer, thanks to rises in world prices of ground nuts, palm kernels and other items of her produce. So she was able to add a further £32 million from her own resources, making a grand total for development of £55 million. It was an exciting prospect. The cheeseparing days were over and Nigeria looked forward to an age of progress. This time, the money was to be fairly and evenly distributed. Development committees were set up in every province to consider needs and make plans. In Sokoto Province the most urgent of these was water. Not only was it scarce all over the province but the water holes and native wells on which most people depended were dirty and ridden with disease. Some stone and cement lined wells had been built in the pre-war era but many more of this type were needed especially in the rural area. A clean pipe-born water system was planned for Sokoto and Birnin Kebbi and in a few years time, there would even be electricity.

Great changes were planned in the medical world also. The hospitals at Sokoto and Gusau were to be much enlarged and a new one was to be built at Birnin Kebbi. Dispensaries already existed in a number of districts, but in certain remoter places, rural health centres were to be set up and staffed by African teams of dispensary attendants, health visitors, sanitary inspectors and midwives. An important part of their job would be to prevent illness by keeping towns and villages clean, by caring for mothers and babies and by vaccinating against the all too familiar scourge of smallpox.

Practically every town would now have a clean and well built market and slaughter house and public latrines would be provided so that people would no longer have to avail themselves of the nearest open space. This, with the plague of flies, had been the main cause of the widespread scourge of dysentery.

The planners then turned their minds to food production. Most farms in Northern Nigeria took the form of small, peasant holdings and these surrounded every town and village. Here each man grew millet, groundnuts, cotton etc., for his family and a surplus to sell at the market. In this way, he raised enough money to pay his taxes and to buy such extras as bicycles, oil lamps and manufactured cloth, for he probably did not clothe his family entirely on homespun cotton. If the rains were plenteous and well-spaced, life was easy but a drought could mean hunger and I had already seen how serious this could be.

So the most important item on the agricultural programme was irrigation. Dams would be made and wells driven by windmills built to provide the necessary water.

Rice was grown in river valleys but it was necessary to hack up the sun-baked swamp clay during the dry season, and that was a slow and back breaking task. So, to help increase rice-production the NA would now have sufficient funds to buy a number of heavy tractors from the United Kingdom.

The upland soil was so soft and light as the marsh clay was heavy. The trouble here was that the earth tended to be blown away by dry season winds or washed off by torrential rains. Sokoto already had too many stretches of bare rock, riddled with gulleys, where there had once been farmland. The battle against this erosion had been fought continuously by the Forestry and Agricultural Departments ever since the early years of British rule. Now, thanks to development funds, far more trees could be planted to protect the exposed farmlands.

Much of the wealth of the country lay in its livestock, most of which was owned and grazed by the nomad Fulani, but thousands of the animals died every year of epidemic diseases such as rinderpest. The Veterinary Departments already carried out immunisation schemes to help the Fulani but now these could be greatly enlarged and made more effective. It was also planned to build a large animal hospital in Sokoto.

Lastly, but most important, came education. Compared with the other regions, the North was extremely backward. From the beginning, Christian missions had run 90 per cent of the schools in the South. But in the North missions were only allowed to operate in pagan areas and the southerners' quarters of the towns; for when Lugard took control of the Northern Emirates, he had promised that the British would not interfere with the Muslim religion. Attempts to do so would in any case have aroused so much resentment as to cause bloodshed. So the educational burden fell largely on the government and the NAs whose revenues were nowhere near adequate to bear it. There were, it is true, Koran schools in every town and village but these taught little except Arabic script and the Muslim faith.

Though Sokoto had some of the best-run Native Administrations in the North, educationally, the province was the most neglected. Up to 1948, only 4,000 Northern children in Sokoto attended schools. This worked out at fifteen children out of every thousand. Of these, a third were girls. Lack of funds was not the only trouble. There was also a devastating lack of public interest in education. However, by 1948, glimmerings of enthusiasm were beginning to show. The chiefs and leading men had always seen the value of education and had set an example by sending their own children to school. Now, a much larger section of the community was following their lead. The younger members of the ruling class were even beginning to show a preference for educated brides. Some of the Council members had to make regular visits to the Sokoto Girls' Training Centre in the course of their duties and found themselves taking a more than academic interest in certain pupils. Certainly two of the Sardauna's charming wives were educated there.

There were forty-six mixed government primary schools spread out in various parts of the province, but the Middle School was for boys only. The pupils entered at thirteen and left at about seventeen. If they completed the course they left with a standard of education about two years below the ordinary level of the (then) British GCE. The best Middle School pupils were selected half way through the course and sent to Kaduna College which was a full secondary school, but there were rarely more than three of four entrants from Sokoto each year. Girls were trained as teachers at the Girls' Training Centre, but a boy who wanted to teach there had to travel 500 miles to the only (Muslim) Teacher Training College at Bauchi.

So, since most other schemes depended on it, the first item in the Education Development Plan was to establish a Teacher Training Centre in the Province. Next, it was planned to raise the standard of the Middle School and to double its intake. Thirdly, three new primary schools would be opened at once and the existing ones expanded. Several more were planned as soon as teachers were trained. Lastly, English would in future be taught at primary schools, for in the past all lessons had been given in Hausa.

Before I returned to England, the Sultan invited Bryan and me to his palace in the town. 'I am always coming to see your house,' he said, 'now it's time that you brought Uwargida to see me.' So we arranged to call on him the following afternoon. We were conducted, as usual, into the Sultan's Council Chamber, a lofty, mud-built hall with thick, white-washed walls on which hung portraits of the Royal Family. The Sultan sat on a red velvet seat with gilded arms and we were motioned to similar ones facing him. We exchanged the customary salutations and talked for a little while. Then he said, 'Perhaps Uwargida would like to see my house.' An elderly woman appeared and led me through a maze of dark passages. Presently, to my great surprise, I found myself in the women's quarters. The Sultan's four wives were there to greet me. They were slim, graceful Fulani girls wearing head veils and swathed garments of indigo cloth striped with white and red. For oranments they had silver earrings and necklaces and beadwork bangles. They smiled at me and clapped their hands in welcome. I was taken into the apartment of each wife in turn, beginning with that of the Uwargida, the Chief wife. The rooms were decorated with handwoven embroidered draperies and with collections of china arranged on shelves. I had a little conversation with each wife before being handed on to the next, and I was given a small present; bangles from one and rings from another, similar to those they were themselves wearing. I was a little confused, for Bryan was always telling me never to accept gifts. However, I did not want to offend them and this did seem to be a special occasion.

Right up to the time I left Nigeria for England, I was still undecided about the wisdom of bringing the children out with me the next tour. However, all doubts were dispelled when I actually saw them. Instead of the rosy-cheeked healthy children I had expected, they were pale and thin. Michael was recovering from two severe attacks of influenza. Geoffrey had chronic tonsillitis and a grumbling middle ear infection. This became acute a fortnight after my return and he was rushed off to hospital for operations on both ears. No sooner had he recovered than he went back to hospital to have his tonsils removed. Perhaps some strong Nigerian sun might even do them good! It seemed, at any rate, worth a trial, for we should all be so much happier together.

Six months later, Angela was born, so when I eventually flew back to Nigeria, I had three children with me. We arrived at Kano and spent a night at the Residency, where the acting Resident also had his three children. Nevertheless, some eyebrows were raised at the 'folly' of taking mine to Sokoto. The last administrative officer's child there had died of cerebral malaria. However, as he had been in Sokoto in the rains when mosquitoes abounded and mine would be there in the dry season when they did not, I remained optimistic. Also, the health conditions had much improved since this tragedy. In fact, although our three were rather thin, they kept fit and they were happy.

Michael and Geoffrey's special joy was being taken on evening duck shooting expeditions to the marshes. As sunset drew near, a sound of whirring wings showed that the birds were taking off from the lakes. Soon they rose in a cloud from amongst the reeds and spread in formation across the sky, calling to one another. Next came the exciting moment when shots rang out from the guns hidden amongst the bushes and those duck which were hit plummeted down, hitting the hard earth with a thud. The moment word was given, our two sons tore after the shot birds, picked them up and carried them, warm and bleeding, to a messenger who was ready with a knife to cut the throats of any that still breathed. But the Sokoto duck were elusive and we seldom bagged more than three or four in an evening.

As soon as it was dusk, we made for the waiting Land Rovers and were soon bumping along on our way home. Lamps twinkled in the marsh villages as we passed. There was a mixed fragrance of wood smoke and cooking as pots of vegetable soup simmered and flaps of meat on sticks sizzled for the villagers' evening meal. Just before entering Sokoto city we had to cross a bridge over the river. It was guarded by a friendly lunatic in a rather tumbled turban and gown who always greeted us effusively and beckoned us over. He was called 'Sarkin Gada' which means the 'king of the bridge' and, to please him, the authorities had presented him with a heavy metal badge to wear on a ribbon round his neck. This was typical of their kindness towards mentally sick people, whom they called 'the afflicted of Allah'.

Michael was by this time seven years old and had already spent two years at the preparatory school at Warwick where the Emir of Abuja had visited him. To continue his education while he was in Sokoto, a young Mallam was found to give him lessons in the usual subjects plus some local history and geography. Mallam Bello and Michael soon became devoted friends and Michael learnt many strange folk tales as the two went together for walks or sat on the rocks and talked.

Geoffrey, then aged three, was happy amusing himself with bricks, sand and watering cans. It was not safe for him to play alone in the garden because of the danger of snakes and scorpions. Being well camouflaged, they were all too easy to come upon unawares. However, Audu, our head servant, was devoted and watchful, and from him Geoffrey learnt some of the mysteries of Africa. Nothing could be more fascinating for a three-year-old than the ant lion for instance, a tiny, dung-coloured creature about the size of a currant. It made a trap in the sand, a cone shaped depression, then hid under the apex and waited. It was fun to speed up matters by finding an ant, dropping it in and watching the disturbance. Alternatively, you could tickle the bottom of the depression gently with a twig and watch the ant lion try to grab it.

Angela spent most of her time in her playpen or cot. She grew steadily and thrived, although, because of the heat, there were feeding problems. When she was nine months old, we were packing again, for Bryan had been appointed Resident, Kano. We were neither of us very pleased, though this was promotion. He would now be the most Senior Resident in the North and would have to 'act' as Chief Commissioner at Kaduna whenever 'His Honour' was away. We had hoped to stay at Sokoto until retirement. However, the sad day at last came when we had to say 'Goodbye'. Bryan left first by road with the boys and I followed the next day by air with Angela. The Sultan and his Council assembled at the airport to wish us farewell and as we rose into the air and I looked through the port hole at our waving friends, I knew that life would never be quite the same again. But in time, we came to love Kano too.

11 KANO RESIDENCY

A very different Kano awaited us from the one we had known in our war days inside the city. The Residency was two miles away, in a European suburb called Nassarawa. Between it and the city was a large, commercial area where British, French, Greek and Indian firms had their stores and warehouses. Adjoining this, in one direction was the Syrian and Lebanese quarter and in the other the '*Sabon Gari;*, or 'New Town', which housed thousands of southerners. A further extension of the township was devoted to Christian missions of different denominations. Each was set at a decent distance from the next and had its own church, school and row of neat houses. The American Baptist Mission boasted of an excellent Eye Hospital, with specialist staff and up-to-date equipment, the only one in the North. Beyond the missions, a short distance into the country, was the International Airport with all its ancillary buildings and hotel.

The retiring Resident of Kano was Mr Featherstone, or 'Feathers' as he was known to his friends. He was still in the Residency when we arrived, but his belongings were packed into crates awaiting despatch to England. Kano was sorrowful to be losing Feathers and a series of multi-racial parties were held to bid him godspeed. These also served to introduce us to Kano society. After the small and unsophisticated community of Sokoto, it was rather overwhelming suddenly to be confronted with hundreds of strange names and faces all to be connected and memorised.

Ever since the days when Kano had been the terminus of the Saharan caravan routes, it had always been a city of traders. In 1950, the general managers of the big commercial firms were so important that they were jestingly referred to as the 'Merchant Princes'. Most of them lived in modern, well furnished houses not far from the Residency. We already knew several and had been entertained by them when passing through on our way to Minna or Sokoto.

The old Emir, who came to tea with us at Gidan Shettima, riding a white donkey, still lived and often visited the Residency. Though he now arrived in a large American car and had his favourite son, the Chiroma, with him. The younger man was not much like his father in appearance. He was taller and more slender and rather grandly dressed. Unlike the shy and thoughtful Emir, he was outgoing and self-assured.

The Residency was an imposing building, rather Moorish in design. It had two storeys and a flat, turreted roof. Deeply arched balconies made the interior cool and shady. The walls were pebbled and painted white, though heavy deposits of harmattan dust had given it a rather grey appearance. The Resident's Union Jack flew from a small tower on the roof.

The garden was shaded by tall mahogany trees, the haunt of plantain eaters during the day and of tree bears at night. The plantain eaters were large brown birds with long tails. They scuttled up and down the branches of the trees and chattered. At night time they were silent and the tree bears gave tongue. Their call was a series of agonised groans, ending in a shriek! For many years we believed that this gruesome noise was made by some eerie night bird and it was a great surprise to discover that it came from so inoffensive a little animal. The tree bear was soft and brown and no larger than a tail-less squirrel and it lived in holes in the trees, only emerging at night.

Beneath the mahoganies were gravel paths, lined with low walls on which pot plants were ranged. Plumbagos, roses and carnations grew in the flower beds which were assiduously watered by the two gardeners. Unfortunately, water was too scarce to stretch to the lawns, which became bald and sandy in the dry season.

At the entrance to the Residency garden, there was a 'Liar' bush, so called because it deceived by growing leaves at one time of year and flowers at another. At the time we arrived the flowers were out, bright pink and star-shaped. Its trunk and stumpy branches were covered with smooth, silver bark and contained a noxious, milky juice. From the entrance to the house there was a drive, which widened as it approached the building. This is where the guns were placed, the pride of the Residency. One was a mountain gun, a relic of Lugard's campaigns, the other two were cannon, each engraved with an 'N' for Napoleon. They had originally belonged to a French expedition which had been given the task of acquiring for France the territories of Adamawa and Bornu, afterwards included in Nigeria, and of Bagirmi, which later formed part of the French colony of Tchad. The party established itself at the capital of Adamawa, but retreated before the advancing British troops. However, it was the Emir who took possession of the cannon and used them against a British occupying force. On the defeat of this Emir, the guns came into British hands and so found their way to Kano.

The upstairs balconies of the house made perfect sleeping out places in the dry season, though the first we chose was unfortunate. It faced the kitchen, which protruded from the rear of the house and was of one storey only. When the cook lit the kitchen range at six o'clock the next morning, the prevailing wind veered and a column of black smoke poured heavily in our direction. We had to get up quickly or be kippered.

Kano was not quite as hot as Sokoto and, indeed, it could be quite cold at Christmas when the harmattan blew, thickly laden with Saharan dust and obscuring the sun. Yet, in the hot season, high temperatures seemed to linger in this large urban area long after the country surrounding the town had been cooled by early showers. Each night, we hopefully watched puff-ball clouds assemble on the eastern horizon only to disperse later. All that would remain of the storm that never came was a soughing wind which billowed the mosquito nets so violently in the middle of the night as to detach them from the beds. They flapped round our faces until we woke up, tucked them in and tried to go to sleep again. The wind would then drop as suddenly and completely as it had started and we would wake once more, pouring with perspiration. Everyone slept out at this time of year. If you passed through the Syrian quarter early in the morning, every balcony, no matter how narrow, seemed to have beds and mosquito nets on it.

To make matters worse, the following year, the Ramadan fast coincided with the hot weather. Abstaining from food and drink through the hours of daylight did not improve people's tempers and Kano was never a tranquil city. Its cosmopolitan nature saw to that.

One Sunday afternoon, a messenger rushed up to the Residency on his bicycle with the news that Kano's only indoor cinema, the 'El Duniya' was on fire. Never dreaming that anyone was inside the building, but to see what was being done to prevent the fire from spreading, Bryan jumped into his car and drove down to the site. To his horror, on arrival at the blazing building, he saw some men, apparently crawling on all fours out of one of the exits. As he drew closer, he saw that they were dead, and that many more corpses were inside. The Kano police were outside, trying to move to the hospital those who had escaped in time and were still alive by stopping passing cars and every other vehicle available.

The fire had started in the projection room during the afternoon performance. More than four hundred people were present, mostly youths. As soon as the audience was aware of the fire, they rushed for the doors. However, it only smouldered at first and after a few minutes, many returned to the building to ask for their money back and to collect their bicycles. Unfortunately, the Syrian owner of the cinema had stuffed the ceiling with a thin type of kapok mattress as a sound-proofing measure. As soon as these mattresses caught fire, the blaze spread like wildfire and burning lumps of kapok dropped on to those still inside the building. The pile of corpses blocking the exits was evidence of the panic which had ensued.

Bryan returned to the Residency and told me this story and later that evening we telephoned the city hospital to ask if we could help in any way. The reply was an emphatic 'Yes'. The hospital was inundated with casualties. Volunteers from the Red Cross and the missions were helping but many more were needed. We arrived at the hospital a few minutes later, but it was some time before we found anyone in authority to tell us what to do. The first ward we entered had a fire victim on every bed and some on mattresses on the floor but no one was attending them. The second ward was the same and it was not until we entered the third that we found a sister at work with two missionaries. We were handed bandages and dressings and given directions. The patients were in great pain, large areas of skin having been destroyed, but they did not complain and made no sound except to thank us for our efforts. An American doctor from the Eye Hospital was giving morphine injections moving fairly rapidly from ward to ward, and two Roman Catholic priests were also circulating, comforting the dying members of their church. We did not see the Medical Officer. He and a number of the nurses were busy all the time in the operating theatre.

When we all came back to help the next day, we found a crowd of the victims' relations waiting outside the hospital wall for news. They had kept vigil all night and were by now frantic with anxiety. At first they had been allowed inside the hospital but as their numbers increased it became impossible to allow them to stay. So before we went home, Bryan addressed them from one end of the wall and suggested that I should do the same at the other. We spoke in Hausa and did our best to reassure them that the doctors and nurses were doing their utmost to save the lives of their relations and that they would give them news as soon as they could.

By the third day, our help was no longer needed. All but fifty of the patients had died. The death toll numbered over three hundred. When the magnitude of the *El Duniya* disaster was revealed, memorial services were arranged in all places of worship. Then came the official enquiry, which blamed the Syrian owners of the cinema.

It so happened that a small group of Northern political extremists had founded a political party and were publishing a newspaper, called the *Comet*, in Kano. They saw, in the *El Duniya* fire, a wonderful change to make sensational headlines. Their leader the next day not only blamed the owners of the cinema but Dr Smith, the Medical Officer of Health, as well. They maintained that he should have detected the dangerous kapok mattresses, which were hidden in the ceiling, during his routine inspection of the building. Nerves were frayed and the *Comet* was after the doctor's blood.

As it happened, Dr Smith was not in Kano at the time but was fulfilling a life-long dream of crossing the Sahara by car. Months ahead, he had bought a desert truck and fitted it for this purpose. He planned to include a friend in the party, with his wife and child. Pressure of work had unfortunately caused the doctor to delay his departure. He had intended making it in the cool weather of February, but by the time he was able to get away it was May. The French authorities had officially closed the route because of the danger of intense heat and sandstorms, so he was travelling at his own risk.

All went well for the first few days. But by the time they had passed through the old city of Agadez and were crossing the most desolate part of the desert, Dr Smith's friend suddenly collapsed of heat stroke and died. The party went back to Agadez, where the dead man was buried, and then returned to Kano. On arrival, they were greeted with the news of the *El Duniya* disaster and of the *Comet's* accusations. The doctor was by this time in a state of acute exhaustion and a fortnight later he, too, died of a stroke.

At last the rain came. Here patches of lawn in the Residency garden turned into pools and, as the water soaked in and the sun came out, delicate blades of grass appeared which soon became strong and dense. Farmers feverishly planted seed in the soft tilled earth which had been barren sand only the week before. Water began to trickle once more through the dried up beds of the rivers.

Now that we had exchanged the simple life of Sokoto for the busy social round of Kano, it seemed essential that a nanny be added to the establishment. Few Northern girls were sufficiently educated in the ways of a white household to be much use but a CMS school for orphans in Zaria was said to train likely candidates. We applied to the church authorities and in due course a Christian Hausa girl named Florence was despatched by train from Zaria to Kano. She was a plump girl of seventeen and arrived wearing a tight pink dress. We had her fitted for a nanny's uniform and she was given a hut in the servant's quarters. From the start, Florence was allowed to wheel the baby out in her pram and to do the infant's washing. Unfortunately, her education had not included ironing and she was too proud to allow Audu to show her how to do it. To make matters worse, she quarrelled with his wife, Abu. Abu had kindly undertaken to cook her food and was annoyed because she quite often failed to appear at meal times. But it was 'followers' in the end that proved the major problem. They had a habit of walking boldly into the Residency grounds by the front entrance, dressed in European-type clothes and claiming to be her brothers. One ended by being caught climbing over the wall, which surrounded the servants' huts, in the middle of the night. This caused no mean stir for burglaries of servants' belongings were common in Kano and would-be seducers of their wives no less so. After the rumpus caused by this incident, we realised that Florence must go, and we managed without a nanny afterwards.

Audu had been our head steward since Minna days. He was a thin man of medium height with a thoughtful face. Before coming to us he had for many years been the valued head servant of a bachelor district officer. Rather late in life, this DO married a pretty London girl, who took a dislike to Audu's beard and told him to remove it. A beard has a special significance to a Muslim and Audu was devout, so he refused and left.

Audu came from a cattle-owning Fulani family which farmed just west of Sokoto. As a boy, he had attended a Koran school so he was well versed in religion and could read and write in Arabic script. He later taught himself to write in English while working as a domestic servant with Europeans. When with his previous master, he had lived in Adamawa where he had married Abu. She was a Fulani girl with skin the colour of creamy coffee. The

Adamawa Fulani were all fair-skinned compared with those from Sokoto. She bore him two fine sons, Saidu and Ali. When the younger one was about seven or eight months old, I often used to watch her, with some sympathy trying to teach the baby to take solid foods. Ali fought and protested and the guinea corn porridge she was trying to make him swallow flew all over the place and dribbled down his mouth, but she persisted. Abu was a determined mother. While we were in Sokoto, she became pregnant again. Miss Cooper, the Nursing Sister, lived next to the Residency and promised to help when the baby came. But Abu was confident. 'I have had two without any trouble', she said firmly, 'this time I will manage by myself.' So when her pains started, she gave no warning until too late. It was about five in the afternoon. Bryan and I had gone off for an evening stroll. By the time we came back, we heard that the gardener had delivered her. I often wondered if he had thought of washing his hands. At all events, the child was dead.

When Abu was expecting her next baby, we were in Kano. This time she promised to be sensible and go into hospital. Unfortunately, soon after we had left for England with the children, Abu became seriously ill with food poisoning and when the baby arrived she had still not fully recovered. If only we had been in Kano, we could have made a personal contact with the Medical Officer which we always did when a servant or a member of his family needed special attention. As it was, the baby was born in hospital but shortly after Abu developed a high temperature. Despite this and protests from Audu, she was discharged and sent home the next day. She became much worse overnight, so Audu took her back to the hospital. A large number of patients were waiting to be admitted and Audu, realising that his wife's case was urgent, offered a bribe which he could ill afford, to the male nurse-in-charge so that Abu could be seen quickly by the doctor. The nurse accepted the money but made her wait her turn. Before it came, the doctor put his head round the door and said, 'I can't see any more patients to-day. Tell them to come back tomorrow.' So Audu took Abu home and she died during the night.

Audu was still distraught when we arrived back from leave about two months later. A man with a family could not manage without someone to cook his food and look after his children. So he had remarried. But he had no love for his new wife and was not particularly surprised when she refused to look after Abu's baby, for the child had survived. With much difficulty, he found foster parents for the baby in the village about three miles away. He bought a European type of feeding bottle and a teat and the foster mother was using this to feed the child with cow's milk, undiluted and unboiled. When I first saw the baby, she was three months old and seemed to be doing fairly well. But two months later she was brought to see me in a very poor state, suffering from acute diarrhoea. 'You must take her to see the Health Sister at the Clinic', I told Audu, but he replied, 'No, I cannot do that because the foster parents will not agree. If I insist they will refuse to keep the child.' I pleaded, 'But if your baby does not have attention, she will die.' Audu's reply was, 'It is the will of Allah. Motherless babies always die.' I telephoned the Health Sister and told her the story. She at once offered to visit the foster parents at the village. Rather to my surprise, Audu agreed to this and thanks to the sister's ministrations, the baby was soon well again. Though the foster parents were simple peasants and illiterate she was able to teach them how to prepare feeds from powdered milk and to sterilise the bottle and teat. Soon the baby was also taking drops of palm oil and tomato juice, inexpensive local equivalents of cod liver oil and orange juice. The baby's name was *'Talle'* but we called her 'Tilly'. She grew into a pretty child with Audu's thoughtful eyes and Abu's fair skin. She and Angela often played together when they were both a few years older.

During our second tour in Kano, we had to contend with a constant stream of visitors from overseas travelling by air. 'Development' was in fullswing and most of the major schemes needed the advice of experts from the United Kingdom. Along with these experts came Members of Parliament, trades union officials and journalists, for Nigeria was becoming world news. One day, a reporter from Chicago walked boldly into the Residency, stumbling over the children's toys. A lanky man in a light blue palm-beach suit, he had a large camera dangling from one shoulder. He must have sensed that I was vexed at his intrusion, for he turned on all his trans-Atlantic charm. He just could not find the Resident. Did I know where he was? Bryan was out, but when he came back he sent the American off on a tour of the city with one of his tougher district officers, an Australian. The Chicago reporter's curiosity about Kano was evidently satisfied, for we did not hear from him again.

Actually, we were only too eager to interest overseas visitors in the country. The North was not generally understood either in Britain or America, where it tended to be regarded as a feudal backwater, quite different from the 'progressive and democratic' South. This was partly because there were already many Nigerian students at overseas universities and colleges from the South but scarcely any from the North.

So many official visitors arrived at Kano airport that it became impossible to entertain them all at the Residency. The district officers and their wives co-operated nobly but their limit was also before long reached. All were busy people and there was much touring to be done in the Province.

Of course we were given advance warning of the arrival of 'very distinguished' guests and entertained them at the Residency. Into this category came Lady Mountbatten, Chairman of the Joint Committee of the British Red Cross and St John's Ambulance Brigade; who charmed us all and particularly the children Archbishop Mathew, the Roman Catholic Apostolic Delegate to Africa, and the Naval Commander-in-Chief of the South Atlantic, Admiral Sir Herbert Packer with his wife, Joy Packer, the writer. But there were many who did not have VIP status but whose mission to Nigeria was nevertheless of the utmost importance. Sometimes we were given warning of them through government sources but many arrived unannounced and we had to rely on the airways officials to keep us informed. In the end, St Elmo Nelson, the Australian DO, was appointed to look after overseas guests, more or less as a whole-time job. This DO had served with the Guards in Crete, with the Australian Forces in New Guinea and as a General's ADC, so he was well equipped for the task. He used to appear at the airport no matter what time of day or night, immaculately dressed in a light-coloured tropical suit and with a carnation in his button hole, culled from the Residency garden. Apart from being well nigh indestructible, he was persuasive and diplomatic. As his 'charges' often arrived unexpectedly and at awkward times of day and night, he was given the title of 'DO Crisis'.

Michael was by this time at a prep school in England but he flew out to Kano by himself for the Christmas holidays, though he was only eight. As luck would have it, his aircraft broke down at Tripoli where all London to Kano flights used in those days to refuel. Though BOAC had 'taken good care of him' in the air, there seemed to be no-one on the ground to help young children in transit, travelling by themselves. However, a kind fellow passenger befriended him and shepherded him by the airways bus back to an hotel in Tripoli itself, which was some miles from the airport.

After which, he knew nothing until he woke the next day on a strange bed with his clothes on. He got up and wandered down the corridor, feeling hungry and hoping it was time for breakfast, only to discover that lunch was being served. The kind stranger re-appeared and took Michael on an afternoon's tour of Tripoli. He saw the beach and the Roman remains. By nightfall, the aircraft was repaired and they took off once more. Michael arrived in Kano the next morning jubilant. He produced a piece of Roman marble from his pocket and said, 'We ought to live in Tripoli instead of Kano, Mummy, it's much prettier.'

Five months later, I went on leave with Geoffrey and Angela, Michael by this time having returned himself to school in England. Unfortunately, the day we left, there was a very heavy storm over the Sahara, which we flew into not long after taking off. 'Attention, please,' said the Air Hostess brightly over the loudspeaker. 'We shall be passing through a slight storm for the next ten minutes. Keep your seat belts fastened.' In fact, we were buffeted all over the place for three solid hours. The sky was black and rain pelted against the glass. Violent flashes of lightening became more frequent until they turned into a continuous, flickering glow. Nearly everyone was sick and I certainly should have been had I not been absorbed in tending my young. At last, to our great relief, we flew into fine weather. Peering through my porthole I could just see the desert in the moonlight. The sand was in silver ripples, like a sea shore at low tide. But there was an ominous click on the loudspeaker and our cheerful friend, the air hostess, addressed us again. 'Attention, please. One of the engines has failed. As we have not quite reached half way to Tripoli, the regulations are that we must return to Kano. We expect to arrive at 10.30.' So presently, we were back in the storm which raged unabated. Only we flew lower this time, because of the damaged engine. On went the seat belts and out came fresh paper bags. Several hours later, we were still flying South and it still poured with rain. It was impossible to see where we were. I looked at my watch. It was 11 o'clock. We must surely have passed Kano, so perhaps we were making for Kaduna, or even Lagos, if the fuel sufficed. Another ten minutes passed and we turned. Then we started to lose height. Down and down we went, with nothing to be seen except rain and blackness. At last we touched the ground, bounced, jerked and finally came to a halt. It was Kano after all, but at the first bounce we had burst a tyre.

Bryan had been dining with Douglas Pott, the Senior District Officer, and his wife Mary. A telephone call from the airport had warned him that we were coming back and he and the Potts had driven to the airport to collect us. But half an hour before we were due to arrive, Kano Radio lost contact with our aircraft. Bryan went into the control tower where he kept searching the sky for some sign of us amid the murk. When at last we appeared through a slight break in the clouds, from the wrong direction, and burst a tyre with a loud report on touching the ground, he was naturally distraught. However, we were safe and, soon after, kind Mary Pott was helping me put the children to bed once more in the Residency.

Next day we started our travels again and this time we reached England without incident. By the following afternoon, we were back in Leamington. Yes, the children had grown and indeed they did look rather tired. Never mind, in the fresh English air we should soon be all right again.

Not long after we returned to Kano at the end of this leave, Nigeria made a significant step forward towards self-government. For the first time, elections were held all over the country. The object was to decide the membership of the Houses of Assembly in the three Regional capitals, which were much enlarged. These Houses, in turn, would send representatives forward to Lagos to the central Parliament, which would now be called the 'House of Representatives'. Each 'House of Assembly' was the equivalent of a Regional House of Commons. Two of the Regions, the North and the West, also had a 'House of Chiefs', corresponding to the House of Lords. The Eastern Region alone had no upper house because in its system of Native Administration the Chiefs were much less important than in the other Regions. The House of Representatives was, of course, the principal parliament of the country.

This was also the time when ministerial government was introduced. Nigerian ministers would now take charge of education, public works, transport, health and so forth. They would be placed over the European directors of the corresponding departments which would now be called 'Ministries'.

Yet a further change was a welcome rise in status of the Regions which made them more independent of Lagos. The Chief Commissioner of the Northern Region, Sir Eric Thompstone, was made a Lieutenant Governor and a similar change occurred in the other Regions.

Sir Eric had almost finished his term of office and was about to retire. Although Bryan had deputised for him once, his promotion to Lieutenant Governor was not a foregone conclusion since it was more likely that someone from outside the territory would be chosen for this appointment. So when the news that Bryan was to succeed was received, there was some excitement at Kano. St Elmo Nelson gave an impromptu party in our honour and plied us all with champagne cocktails. It took two glasses of this potent mixture to drown my inward groans at the thought of becoming a Lieutenant Governors' wife and of all the awful formalities of Kaduna.

Sad as we had been to say goodbye to Sokoto two years before, we had by now grown to like the hectic, cosmopolitan life of Kano. But regrets were useless, we must pack again. Sylvia and 'Waddle' Weatherhead would be taking over at the Residency. They had followed us to Sokoto also. Bryan went ahead to Lagos to be sworn in as Lieutenant Governor and I went direct by road to Kaduna. My final ridiculous frustration was when I found that the furniture removal lorry was so tightly packed that there was no room for the pots of rare roses which had been given to me only a few days before by one of our Greek friends.

PART THREE

12 GOVERNMENT HOUSE

After the Residency, Kano, Government House seemed enormous. It was true that the last occupant had been a bachelor and that he had managed with only a male private secretary to help him. All the same, a different standard would surely be expected now that there was a wife.

I need not have been fearful, however, for Government House had an excellent and experienced staff of servants. Joseph, the oldest and most senior, was called the 'caretaker'. He was responsible for all the furnishings of the house, including the linen, glass, china and silver of which there was a large stock. Not long after we moved in, he and I checked all these items with an inventory several years old and the only missing objects were a few teaspoons. It was a remarkable feat of steadfastness on Joseph's part; for all that time he had been conscientiously checking the stores by himself, keeping outworn face towels, pillow slips, broken china etc. to be written off in due course. Apart from his main responsibilities, Joseph arranged the flowers and helped at table whenever there were guests. He was a tall, solidly built Yoruba, clean-shaven and with noble features like those of the famous Ife bronzes. His home town was near Lagos.

Next came Ali Gombe, the head steward or butler. He was a suave Fulani who had acquired polish in one of the larger European households of Lagos. Ali had a neat moustache, rather a pale complexion for a Nigerian and well-cut features. He was amusing, diplomatic and knowledgeable especially in matters of local history and folk lore.

'Little' Ali, so called, not because of his stature, but to distinguish him from the 'greater', i.e. more senior Ali, was a strapping young man with a round face, aged about twenty. He made up in willingness and good temper what he lacked in expertise.

As a personal servant, we still had Audu with us. Fortunately he already knew the Government House staff and was a close friend of Ali Gombe. John, our cook, came with us too. He was a middle aged Ibo, with bandy legs, who knew his job though he had his limitations. As the demands of Government House far exceeded the capabilities of one cook, we acquired a second one, also named John but taller and at least fifteen years younger than his namesake. A third, the 'cook's mate', i.e. apprentice cook, was then engaged to run errands and clean the kitchen.

The head gardener was an elderly man with a thin long beard named Nda, who came from the riverside town of Lokoja. It was his responsibility to organise the work of the five other gardeners and the teams of prisoners who trooped up from the local gaol each morning accompanied by the warder, to cut grass and weed the lawn. As the grounds covered fifty acres, Nda had no easy task but was a born administrator. He commanded his labour force with a rasping voice, heavily laced with sarcasm. However, this rather stern character had an acute sense of humour and when it was tickled his taut features would break into a broad grin.

Of the three chauffeurs, the most outstanding was a heavily-built ex-blacksmith named Alkali. A conversational Kano man, he was a skilful and reliable driver. It was usually he who drove me to morning engagements in various parts of Kaduna, or to the Leper Settlement, a girls' school and a convent which I used occasionally to visit at Kakuri, five miles outside the town. I found him a most likeable person. His gossip was always amusing, sometimes a little tart. He was not so popular with some members of the staff, however. Perhaps this was because much of his work took place after five o'clock, so qualified for overtime and he splashed the extra money about in a rather ostentatious way. For instance, he, alone amongst them, was able to afford to make the pilgrimage to Mecca by air, and he took his senior wife with him.

Audu mai Kano, whom we simply called 'Mai Kano' to distinguish him from the other Audu, was an equally competent driver but with a more unassuming character. The third driver we saw less since he was mainly concerned with the Government House lorry.

Then there was the washerman 'Antony', whose real name was 'Antoine', since he came from French territory, and his mate. There were two or three 'small boys' and a couple of grooms and to complete the picture, there lived in a separate homestead about fifty yards from the other staff huts an elderly Fulani with his

family, whose dark robes and long beard made him look like a
prophet. His job was to care for the Government House oxen.
When the grass grew long in the paddock, which surrounded the
garden, these two white beasts were yoked together to pull a
rickety grass cutter. At other times, they had a less picturesque
function which was to supply the garden with manure. In all,
about forty people lived within the compound, for Government
House was essentially a human institution.

The main building was of pink brick and white cement with two
lofty storeys and a steep, tiled roof. An imposing car porch
projected from the centre of the front. It had pairs of pillars on
either side and a square, flat roof. Balconies ran across the front of
the house on both floors, decorated with 'fret-work' patterns in
cement. Beyond them, at either end, were gables and, at the rear,
a substantial wing projected from one side. This housed the Private
Secretary on the ground floor and principal guests above. At the
extreme end of this wing, there was an interior spiral staircase. As
some of the earlier Chief Commissioners* had tended to retire to
bed early, this stairway had been useful for socially minded guests,
who wanted to slip in late at night after visiting friends without
disturbing their host. We had its top door sealed as a precaution
against thieves, so, though it intrigued the children and provided
sanctuary for the mason wasps, it was otherwise unused.

The house was entered through the car porch and up a flight ofr
rather slippery steps which I always treated with respect as I had
already fallen down them once on a visit to a former Chief
Commissioner. They were painted tomato-red and polished to a
high gloss. At the top of the stairs there was a vestibule, where
portraits of King George V and Queen Mary hung, and this led
into a spacious L-shaped drawing room. At the far end was a wide
bay window, and in the centre, glass doors opened onto the
terrace. Over one of the drawing room's two fireplaces hung a
picture of George VI as an Admiral of the Fleet and over the other
a Cecil Beaton portrait of Queen Elizabeth (now the Queen
Mother) dressed in a diamond-spangled crinoline. On the other
side walls were photographs of King Edward VII as a Field Marshal
and an elegant Queen Alexandria, liberally roped in jewels.

Swing doors on either side of the far fireplace led into the dining-
room, a long, mahogany panelled apartment whose only adorn-

*The Chief Commissioner was later to be called a 'Lieutenant
Governor' then, under the Federal System, 'Governor'.

ment was a sepia-tinted portrait of Queen Victoria. Beyond the dining room was the kitchen wing. Bryan's office and those of his Private Secretary were in a line at the opposite side of the drawing room, a useful retreat during the day time for the children and me. Upstairs were five bedroom suites and a billiard room.

Government House would have been luxurious if the furnishings had been adequate. But the period of wartime austerity had only just ended. Stringent economies in all government quarters had been the rule and our predecessors had set an outstanding example to others. The result was that nearly all the easy chairs had sagging springs and were placed strategically over patches where moths had eaten the carpet or the floor boards were faulty. In such surroundings, all that was needed was a ghost. Ali Gombe was convinced that there was one and it was not long before we, too, noticed mysterious happenings. Lights turned themselves off and on and ceiling fans behaved in the same strange manner. But the cause was revealed a few weeks later when electricians overhauled the wiring. They found that rats had gnawed the insulation off a network of cables in the cellars, causing short circuits. The fuses had then been mended by amateur electricians from amongst the staff with hair pins and any other odd pieces of wire that came to hand. It was fortunate that this had only caused one small fire, for though the house had fire fighting equipment, the water pressure was usually so feeble as to make the hoses useless. St Elmo Nelson, our first Private Secretary, the 'DO Crisis' of Kano days, undertook to test it and, as a result, we had fire extinguishers installed everywhere instead.

It was our luck to arrive at Kaduna at a time of greater government affluence. This made us free to order all the new curtains and carpets which were so badly needed and to have the chairs and floorboards either repaired or replaced. The Ministers were often in and out of the House and they watched developments with a personal and approving eye, for they felt that Government House belonged to them too, as indeed it did.

Any illusions of grandeur which I may have been developing were rudely shaken the first time that Bryan went away on tour, leaving the children and me at home. Normally, there was an armed police guard in full dress uniform on duty at the main entrance to the grounds. Whenever Bryan passed through, the bugler played the General Salute and they all presented arms. After dark, strangers attempting to enter were challenged and only allowed to pass if they managed to satisfy the guard of their bona fides. But, the moment the gubernatorial còrtege departed on tour, leaving me behind, to my consternation the guard pulled down the Union Jack, packed up and departed. Government House was in an isolated position, well away from the residential part of the town, and I did feel very much deserted. However, as Bryan pointed out to me when he returned, there was no real cause for alarm, since there were still two policemen on patrol duty in the grounds and one of them was supposed to keep a watch on the main entrance. Nevertheless, the departure of the gate guard was a signal for a general easing of tension. Office messengers sitting on the steps below my window, pushed their turbans back, scratched their heads, and loudly exchanged the latest jokes and gossip. I had to ask them to be more quiet. When Bryan was working in his office they never raised their voices above a respectful whisper.

That evening, a car drove up to the porch. It was Bryan's second-in-command, the Civil Secretary, Leslie Goble with his wife Mickie. They had telephoned a number of times from their house which was two miles away in the centre of Kaduna. There had been no reply and they wondered if I was all right. Of course I replied that I was perfectly all right but that I had not heard the telephone ring. The messenger in charge of the telephone was called and I was rather wrathful when he replied, 'Oh, I disconnected the telephone. This is what we always do when there is no one in the house!'. The trouble was that the household had for many years been accustomed to a bachelor master and they looked forward to a glorious rest when ever he left on tour. They now had to learn what was right and proper when the Governor's wife and family were in residence during his absence.

Soon after Bryan returned from tour, Sir John and Lady Macpherson, the Governor and his wife, came from Lagos to stay with us. After their first night under our roof, I made the usual polite enquiries about how they had slept. There was a significant pause and then His Excellency said, 'Very well, after four a.m.!' It seemed that several owls had flown into their bedroom, one of which perched on a corner of the mosquito net rail, refusing to move. It was not until four a.m. that our guests had at last been able to dislodge him and drive him out of the window.

Before this episode, we had felt a certain fondness for our owls. They lived beneath the eaves just outside the billiard room window and we used to hear them snoring when we were playing snooker in the evenings. Now we realised that they would have to go. Ali

Gombe drove them from their roost. They flew off and perched in high trees in various parts of the garden. Meanwhile, Bryan fetched and loaded his shot gun. Presently, eleven dead owls fluttered to the ground with a flurry of soft white down and grey feathers. H.E. and Lady M were upset to be the cause of this slaughter but afterwards our guests slept undisturbed and many small and colourful birds came into the garden which had not dared to venture there before.

Kaduna had been chosen as the administrative capital of the North by Lord Lugard at the time of the First World War. Before it had been uninhabited bush. The new capital was named after the river which ran nearby, the word 'Kaduna' meaning 'crocodiles'. Wide roads and avenues crossed one another at right angles, making a geometric pattern, interrupted in the centre by the oval sweep of the race course, the broad, angled ribbon of the golf course and an open area set aside for offices.

The Region's House of Parliament was named after Lord Lugard, the founder of the capital and the first High Commissioner of Northern Nigeria. The Lugard Hall was built at the top of a gentle hill and was approached by an avenue of stately mahoganies. From the outside, it looked more like an oriental place of worship than an official building and was one of the Public Works Departments architectural masterpieces. A wide, white structure, it had a central tower surmounted by a copper dome, on either side of which were wings two storeys high. Its arcades were decorated with concrete tracery. Inside, the main hall was modelled on the House of Commons, with an oblong well in the centre from which the members' benches rose in horse-shoe shaped tiers. The President's throne corresponded with that of the Speaker and faced the assembly from the open end of the horse-shoe. Above hung a Royal Coat of Arms in colour and gilt.

While he was Resident, Kano, Bryan had been the President, i.e. Speaker, of the House of Assembly. Now, as Lieutenant Governor, he held the same position in the House of Chiefs. I often watched sessions of both Houses from the Strangers' Gallery and I was always there for the opening ceremonies. These were performed with much civil and military pomp, the Europeans in uniform or their smartest outfits, the Nigerians in their most colourful gowns. In the evening, we entertained the members to a garden party at Government House and this often ended with a film show. A documentary of the Queen's recent coronation, in colour, was especially popular. Few of the Muslims brought their wives, only the youngest and most audacious. There were some Christians in both Houses and their wives came with them automatically. We always enjoyed these parties and especially meeting old friends such as the Sultan of Sokoto and the Waziri, the Emirs of Kano, Kontagora and Abuja.

Some members of the House of Assembly also belonged to the House of Representatives in Lagos and they used to bewail the fact that they spent so much time between the two capitals that they were scarcely ever at home. One of these was Mallam Abubakar Tafawa Balewa, the Minister of Works. A quiet and serious man, he had once been the headmaster of Bauchi Middle School. Abubakar was already renowned, both as a thinker and as an orator. The Press called him the 'Golden Voice' of the North. Bryan thought a great deal of him and often invited him alone to the house for a talk. Although Abubakar was a commoner and at times a most outspoken critic of the regime, he was listened to with respect by both white officials and the chiefs.

Another ex-middle school headmaster who had risen to fame was the Makama of Bida, a friend since the Minna days, for Bida was in Niger Province. Makama was a neatly-built man with shrewd, smiling eyes and a determined mouth. He was not a man to bother over much with dress, being usually in too much of a hurry; though on ceremonial occasions his turbans and gowns were amongst the richest and most immaculate. Makama was Minister of Education in the Northern Government.

Although Geoffrey and Angela missed Kano at first, they quickly settled into the Government House routine. Geoffrey attended a kindergarten held in the Club each morning, close to the golf course. Angela meanwhile graduated from the playpen to a morning nursery school, run by a police officer's wife. In the evenings we often took the two children to the swimming pool which had originally belonged to the army but was now in general use. It was in shady gardens by the Kaduna river, a favourite resort for parents and children. Little tots learnt to swim as soon as they could walk and it was a common sight to see five year olds scrambling up to the top diving board at the deep end and hurling themselves off, one after another.

Bryan sometimes took Geoffrey by himself on shooting expeditions of an evening, and twice they went together on tour. On one of these occasions, they had been invited by the army to watch anti-bandit exercises at a place called Kachia, seventy miles south of Kaduna. To Geoffrey's great delight, the brigadier allowed him to blow up a bridge. This he did, concealed in a foxhole less than a hundred yards away, by pressing a plunger at the word of command. There was a tremendous bang which sent clouds of dust and debris rocketing into the air and caused three visiting politicians to duck most unceremoniously beneath the nearest lorry. To cap it, on the way down, a magnificent herd of roan antelope crossed the road only just in front of the car.

When Geoffrey was eight years old, he joined Michael at Milner Court, the preparatory school for the King's School Canterbury and the two boys came out to Nigeria by air for the Christmas holidays. Bryan's leave usually coincided with the summer holidays which we all spent together in Englnd and the boys stayed with relatives or at a holiday home for Easter.

Whenever I was pre-occupied with entertaining or with some form of social service, Audu was already ready, if necessary, to take charge of Angela. He was more reliable than any nanny. A small summer house, nor far from the main building, had been converted into a play room and was equipped with a sand pit and doll's house. After a couple of years, Angela outgrew the playroom in this form and it became the headquarters of a Brownie Pack, of which she was an enthusiastic member. The Brownies also had the run of a shady lawn and duck pond, on which swam some live Muscovy ducks. Sometimes, obligingly watching the Brownies from a nearby tree sat a real tawny owl, a survivor of the slaughter.

By this time, there were a hundred or more white children in Kaduna alone. Many parents could no longer afford the expense of keeping their children in the UK while they were in Nigeria. Moreover, new ideas on child psychology stressed the harmful effects of separating young children from their parents. Recently developed anti-biotics dealt swiftly with such debilitating diseases as typhoid and bacillary dysentery and the new anti-malarial medicines were pleasanter to take than quinine and less devastating to the appearance than mepacrine, which made the skin turn yellow. So it was now possible for conscientious parents to keep their offspring reasonably healthy. Nevertheless, although the European children in Kaduna were generally quite fit, they tended to be thin, pale and over active.

During the latter part of our six years in Kaduna, a dream of Makama's became reality. This was the founding of a multi-racial school for the children of African and European officials. He had to fight opposition from his own Ministry on the grounds that such a school would depart from the democratic principles on which

Nigerian education had been founded. However, Makama was not a man to be easily defeated and he had his way. The 'Capital School' as it was called, opened in a disused railway rest house with half a dozen white children and about double that number of Nigerians. Angela was amongst them. Some years later, a boarding house was added to the school which was now housed in a splendid new building and the numbers rapidly grew into the hundreds.

Angela's school friends included Binta and Bala, the children of Abubakar Tafawa Balewa, Fatima, the daughter of Sir Kashim Ibrahim, the daughter of the Emir of Yauri, and the grandsons of the Emirs of Katsina and Kano. They occasionally came to play in our garden at the weekends; a red toy car of Angela's was extremely popular with the boys.

13 GOVERNOR'S WIFE

As the Lieutenant Governor's wife, I was automatically expected to be the President of the Regional Branch of the Red Cross Society and also of the Regional Girl Guides Association. The organisation of the Guide Movement was in the competent hands of the Regional Commissioner, Dr Geary, later to become Lady Alexander, who was also the Assistant Director of Education for Women. All that I had to do was to take the Chair at the Annual Meeting and to appear at Guide functions in festive clothes, with a smile and ready to say a 'few words'. The smile at least was easy, for the girls were such a responsive and cheerful audience.

The Red Cross, however, was a different matter. As President, I was also the Chairman of the Executive Committee which met about every two months and included amongst its members such people as the Attorney General, the Minister of Health, the Director of Medical Services and the Civil Secretary. I felt sure that they knew much more than I did about the conduct of meetings. I approached my first one rather nervously and, with copious notes. The British Red Cross Society in London had posted a field officer to Kaduna and she sat next to me and helped me with the details. One of our first problems was to provide her with living quarters and an office. I had already been firmly told that, since the Red Cross was a voluntary society, we were not entitled to use government buildings. This meant that though we had virtually no funds for the purpose, we should have to build a Red Cross headquarters and furnish it. This was far from easy. The effort had to be region-wide and, especially in the provinces, there was resentment that Red Cross funds should be spent on a building and not directly on the sick and injured. However, with the help of a small loan from London headquarters, the house was approved and built and within eighteen months, Lady Limerick, Vice-Chairman of the British Red Cross Society, came to open it.

Meanwhile, our field officer was spending much of her time on tour. Kano and Plateau Province already had Red Cross Divisions, and were very well established, so her first aim was to form them in the remaining ten provinces. As soon as a fair number of these units were functioning, we started to form more detachments for both men and women. A regional competition was held annually at Kaduna between the detachments. The Army Medical Corps kindly helped us by faking a series of accidents with which the Detachments had to compete and which their CO and his staff helped to judge. As far as detachments were concerned we were well ahead of all the other regions of Nigeria. We were also doing a considerable amount of welfare work for mission hospitals and leper settlements, Junior Red Cross units had been established in a number of the larger schools, and a blood transfusion service was also started in Kaduna.

However, in one important way, our Red Cross work was only partly satisfactory. The vast majority of the members were English-speaking southerners from the *sabon garis* of the main towns or mission-educated Christians from the Middle Belt. We had scarcely a single Muslim woman in the organisation. Of course, we were up against the age old custom of purdah. Most of the womenfolk of the ruling classes were still confined within the walls of their own compounds and excluded from all mixed society. European women were occasionally invited to meet wives in purdah and I myself visited those of the Sultan of Sokoto, the Emirs of Kano, Katsina and Abuja and of the Sardauna, but such contacts were not often allowed. The less well-to-do could not afford to keep their wives locked up, but these women seldom spoke English and were mostly illiterate.

However much we might regret the purdah situation, it was not for us to interfere with the social customs of the country. But we all felt that we ought to make a much greater effort to teach Red Cross techniques in the language of the country. The only available Red Cross manuals were in English and illustrated white people in a European environment. We decided to start by making a Hausa translation of the *First Aid Manual*. Mr Hindle, the Regional Director of Information, was a member of our Executive Committee and promised his full co-operation. More important still, when I put the matter to the ministers they strongly supported the idea and agreed to provide the money. Mr Hindle happened to be a competent amateur artist, so he undertook to prepare the illustrations himself; showing Northern Nigerians in a home setting but keeping the pictures as near as possible to those of the original version. We decided to add the treatment for snake bite and scorpion sting, two common mishaps in Northern Nigeria which were not mentioned at that time in the English manual.

Before our Hausa *First Aid Manual* could become reality, we required the approval of the London Headquarters. Several weeks after we had sent them our draft, we at last had a reply. Instead of the hoped for approval they sent us a new version, which they had recently produced for use in 'coloured' areas. The illustrations showed Red Cross workers and patients of an indeterminate, greyish complexion, whose features varied from negroid to Chinese. None looked at all like Northern Nigerians. The reading matter was in four languages which did not include Hausa though Arabic was amongst them. Although classical Arabic was used in the North in connection with the Muslim religion, the language was not generally understood, except by a few scholors. It was rather like issuing a Latin manual for the use of the British members of the society, and really quite useless. I tried to explain this but London seemed unable to understand why their new afro-asian manual was not acceptable and we remained eager to have our own version.

The correspondence was still dragging on when I left Kaduna for leave. We had just bought a house at Hythe in Kent. It was half-timbered and had roses growing up one side. At last we had a permanent home in England and this was a great thrill for all the family, even though we could only use it for brief periods of leave. I had so much to do, furnishing the new house and preparing it for letting during our absence, that I could not return with Bryan straight away at the end of his leave. So Sarah, his grown-up daughter by his first marriage, went to Nigeria with him and acted as his hostess at Government House while I was away. Scarcely a week passed without one or more interesting official visitors arriving from overseas and I think she found, as I did, that entertaining them was one of the most aggreable aspects of life at Government House. One of her guests was the Secretary of State for the Colonies himself, Mr Lennox-Boyd (afterwards Viscount Boyd) on his first visit to Northern Nigeria.

By this time, an ADC had been added to the establishment for the regions had once more been up-graded in another big step towards self-government. The regional lieutenant governors were now made full governors and Sir John Macpherson became the Governor General, for Nigeria was now a federation. Sardauna was appointed the first Premier of the Northern Region and Alhaji Abubakar Tafawa Balewa two years later became the Prime Minister of the Federation with a permanent official residence in Lagos.

A visible result of the change were the large numbers of new government buildings which sprang up like mushrooms all over the capital. Commercial firms which had hitherto taken little interest in Kaduna as a trading place, now began building new stores. Before, the United Africa Company's Kingsway Stores had been the only one. It was now pulled down and rebuilt as a spacious supermarket.

When I at last returned to Kaduna, work had already also started on the enlargements to Government House which we had previously planned. The dining room extended to double its old length, the kitchen was completely rebuilt and modernised and several new rooms were added. In the grounds, a stark concrete block shot up with shattering speed, mercifully hidden behind a clump of trees. This was the security building, the headquarters of the newly enlarged regional intelligence organisation. It housed the cypher staff who kept us in touch with the rest of the world. In a country the size of Northern Nigeria, which was subject to inter tribal and religious quarrels and feuds between recently formed political parties, civil disturbances could erupt suddenly and dangerously in almost any of the 12 Provinces. A hand-picked administration officer was in charge. A further change to Government House was that the police guard at the main entrance was now replaced by an army guard.

14 THE NORTH ON THE MOVE

Bryan often had to leave Kaduna to tour the provinces, each one of which he tried to visit at least once a year. In this way, he could hear local problems on the spot and ease the feeling of isolation that was common, especially in the more remote provinces. Sometimes these visits had a special purpose such as the installation of a new emir or the presentation of honours, perhaps a CMG, an OBE, or an MBE to people whose names had appeared in the current year's Buckingham Palace Honours Lists. On other occasions, the object was just to meet people and entertain as many as possible. For family reasons, I was not always able to accompany him, but whenever such expeditions coincided with school holidays, I went with delight, taking the children with me. They were so pleased, as I was, to have a change from the enclosed atmosphere of Kaduna.

One of our longest and most interesting tours had been to Kabba Province, over two hundred miles from the capital, and due south of it. John Matthew, the Private Secretary at that time and Jean, his wife came with us. We took the train from Kaduna, via our old home Minna, to Baro, an old port on the River Niger, where two motor launches and a couple of barges awaited us. Our cars were loaded onto the barges, one of the launches was filled with domestic staff and we occupied the other one. As soon as everything was stowed away, our little fleet started its journey down the river which was nearly a mile wide at this point. The banks were deeply fringed with reeds beyond which dark forest was broken from time to time by riverside villages. We passed several dug-out canoes covered with canopies of matting. Each was propelled by two or three Nupe boatmen, stripped to the waist, their muscles rippled beneath gleaming skin as they thrust the poles into the water, leaned on them and then swung them up again, with strong, rhythmic movements. One of the canoes travelling downstream was packed with chickens in cages, another carried a cargo of earthenware bowls and rolls of rush matting.

Those moving upstream appeared to be more lightly loaded and their cargo was mainly under cover. The cargo consisted of manufactured goods from the coastal ports; bales of Manchester cotton, fish hooks, needles and twine for sale at wayside markets.

After four sweltering hours we arrived at a pre-arranged halt on a sand bank on which the village head had prepared a camp, where we were to spend the night. The shelters were made of rush mats tied on to a framwork of poles. We were soon unpacked and by six o'clock, Angela was eating a supper of soup and fried Nigerian perch, which cook had concocted in the galley of one of the launches. John and Jean Matthew had meantime gone to explore the mainland and Bryan had departed in a stubby, metal dinghy belonging to the launch to try his hand at fishing. He took a marine deck hand with him and one of the local boatmen. Much time passed. The sun disappeared beneath the horizon and the boys lit the oil lamps. Soon the stars came out and it was quite dark. Angela was by this time settled into her camp bed and there was no noise except the muted hum of the boys' conversation and the lapping of water round the boats. I looked at my watch. It was already eight o'clock. Bryan had left at half-past four. Surely he should have returned by this time. Another half-hour passed and I began to feel very alarmed. At last I heard a shuffling in the sand behind me. It was Bryan, speechless with exhaustion. When he regained his breath, he began to tell me the story.

Never doubting the ability of his crew to manage the dinghy, the had dropped a long way down stream. But the fish refused to bite, so he had decided to give up and come back. There was a pause while he finished the stiff whiskey and soda which I had mixed for him. Then he continued his tale. 'It wasn't until the boatmen turned the dinghy into the current that I realised they knew nothing about paddling. Or at any rate, they couldn't paddle that awkward little tub. It kept swinging from side to side and all the time we were being swept further downstream. I was sitting in the stern and doing my best to balance the boat. After a bit, I siezed one of the paddles and managed to keep the dinghy head on to the current. Then I got the less incompetent of the two boatmen to help and foot by foot we began to make headway'. After striving for well over an hour, they at last reached the southern tip of the island, where Bryan had dragged himself ashore. The last few hundred yards, he continued on foot clambering wearily through the soft powdery sand to where I was anxiously awaiting him.

It was fortunate that the boat had returned safely for this part of the river was full of crocodiles. We saw them on the banks the next day, sunning themselves, with their great jaws wide open.

The first official port of call was Lokoja, the capital of Kabba Province and the old-time capital of the North. The town sloped gently up from the river. Behind it, on a series of uneven rocky terraces, there was a largely European residential area. Slightly upstream, was a range of steep hills densely covered with trees and on the opposite side of the river, distant mountains shimmered pink in the midday heat.

The Residency, where we spent the night, was the 'twin' of the new Residency in Sokoto, so we felt instantly at home. The Resident was a distinguished looking Irishman with a monocle. His attractive French wife and six-year-old step-son were with him. The little boy's own father had been killed in a car accident in Nigeria only two years before and the child still seemed rather stunned. He said that he was a French boy and did not want to speak English, so, when he had supper with Angela in the nursery there was not much conversation. But the Resident and his wife did their utmost to make us comfortable and despite the sticky climate we enjoyed our visit and were sorry to move on the next day. We left, quite early in the morning, by road for Okene, headquarters of one of the divisions. The road took us through wooded country winding upwards. As we drew near our destination, the trees gave way to mountain scenery with craggy hills and deep, fertile valleys. A reservoir had been made above Okene in a cleft between the hills. There was a small island in the centre where willowy gum trees were reflected in the water. An old boat, half filled with rain water, lay beside the wooden jetty. The lake had been plentifully stocked with fish and later that afternoon Angela caught several on a simple hook and line, much to her delight.

The houses of Okene town were more ambitious in design than was usual in the north. Although built of mud bricks, many were two-storeyed. No doubt they were safer than they appeared to be, but those that were still only half-finished looked as though a determined push would cause them to collapse. The people were prosperous, judging by their clothes, and I later discovered a high rate of literacy.

We stayed overnight at the district officer's house and left the next day for a brief visit to the old town of Kabba, only a few miles from the border between the Northern and Western Regions. There we met the chief and some of his people. They talked about the politicians from across the border who were casting predatory eyes on Kabba and were doing their best to stir up trouble.

In the afternoon, we returned to the river where the launches were waiting to take us on to the port of Idah. Soon after we cast off, we were astonished to see a column of oily black smoke, apparently rising from the middle of the bush. However, when we turned a deep bend in the river, we discovered that it came from an ancient stern wheeler which was ploughing its way upstream.

As we approached Idah, we were met by a reception committee in brightly decorated dug-out canoes. The crew were singing, beating drums and jiving with such vigour that I expected a boat to capsize at any minute. The chief, who was called the 'Ata', and the district officer were waiting for us, at the landing stage. The chief was a pagan, but he wore the usual turban and gown of a Muslim emir. As soon as the cars had been off-loaded, we were escorted through the town and up a hill to a bluff overlooking the river. Here, a newly-built house had been prepared for us, not far from where the DO lived. Thanks to luxuriant vegetation and particularly to the groves of fruitful palm trees, Idah people were vigorous and well-fed. Yet, despite this and the gaiety of our reception, we soon began to notice a brooding atmosphere which seemed to hang over the town.

The Ata had once been one of the more promising and enlightened of the younger chiefs but, as the years passed, he had fallen under the influence of a sinister clique of old men from amongst his own councillors. They had reverted to certain unpleasant customs which included drug-taking, sex orgies and the torture of animals. The Ata himself was known to have become a drug addict. In olden times, a virgin had been sacrificed each year and it was rumoured that this ritual had been secretly revived. The story had even reached the Lagos press.

Many of the younger generation had been educated in mission schools and they resented being ruled by this sordid tyranny. Amongst their leaders was a tall, heavily-built man named Peter Achimugu. He had started life as a steam roller driver in the Public Works Department, but an interest in local politics had taken him to the House of Assembly and now he was a minister in the Northern government. At first the older Muslim ministers were reluctant to agree to the inclusion of such men as Achimugu. But as soon as they got to know this kindly and gifted Christian, they changed their minds and accepted him as one of themselves. 'Mr Peter', as he came to be known, and his supporters in Idah, were naturally not willing to tolerate the Ata and his ways much longer and as soon as we returned to Kaduna, steps were taken to prepare for a change.

In the meantime, we continued our tour, giving evening receptions wherever we went to the leaders of society both black and white. We brought all the equipment with us, including glasses, drinks, and the raw materials for the savouries and it was quite an undertaking for the Alis, great and small, to unpack and prepare for these occasions from our touring loads and then wash and pack again before repeating the process at the next port of call.

Idah was, in fact, the last stop on our itinerary in the Northern Region. Our party there was marked by a violent thunderstorm which broke just as guests were filing in. The front path of our house was rapidly converted into a mighty torrent and, presently, all the lights went out so that, until the boys had groped for oil lamps and lit them, we were plunged into darkness.

The following day, we took the road eastward to Enugu, a hundred miles away, crossing the frontier between the Northern and Eastern Regions. Enugu, being the capital of the Eastern Region, was the seat of the Lieutenant Governor, Sir Clem Pleass, and we stayed the night at his Government House, a pleasant and relaxing change after all our travels. Bryan and Clem were quickly deep in conversation about their various problems, while Sybil Pleass showed me her lovely garden and thriving English poultry, which were her special pride. She used to order day-old chicks from the United Kingdom which came out by air freight. These were kept at an even temperature in a spare wardrobe with a heater fitted, until the chicks were sufficiently established to withstand the rigours of the Enugu climate. Not that, as far as human beings were concerned, it was particularly rigorous. In fact, it was warm and sticky most of the time. The wardrobe heater was a customary fitting in all humid places and was intended to prevent mildew forming on clothes.

We returned, reluctantly, to Kaduna the next day by air.

A few weeks after our return, a meeting of chiefs was called, which the Ata was not expected to attend. He had already been told that because his people had rejected him, the government could no longer recognise him as their chief. However, he arrived in Kaduna, so Bryan called him to Government House and repeated the message, insisting that he must retire.

That evening, the usual reception was held at Government House and, to our consternation, the Ata drove up in his car with the other chiefs as though nothing had happened. He was evidently living in a dream world and had simply not taken in the fact that he had been politely sacked. At all events, when I saw him coming towards me that night with a glassy expression on this face, I could not think what to say to him and was overcome with dismay. On his way back to Idah that night by car, he hanged himself on a tree.

The next time we went to Kabba Province, the new Ata was installed. He was an educated young man and a convert to Islam and one of his first acts was to abolish the more barbarous of the pagan practices of his predecessor.

The next major event was the opening of the Institute of Administration at Zaria, an ancient city about fifty miles to the North of Kaduna. The Zaria of old had been the capital of one of the original Hausa States, and like Kano, was a city of mud-brick architecture, encircled by a high wall, but a number of new buildings had recently been erected, including several colleges and a large printing press. Zaria was rapidly becoming the major cultural centre of the North.

The Institute was developed from the old Clerical Training College where for some years past, northerners had been trained as clerks so as to take over at least some of the posts then usually occupied by southerners. This college was now re-named and re-built and its scope enlarged to include courses for those already occupying responsible jobs. Some were for emirs' councillors, treasurers and scribes, others for the chiefs themselves, and there was even one for the assistant district officers. Many experienced men gladly availed themselves of opportunities of learning new and more efficient techniques in local government. A few years later, as the country moved towards independence, the Institute began to train Northern Nigerians as administration officers and police officers. This was so successful that visitors from all over the world came to see it and it became a model for other emergent countries in Africa.

The Governor, Sir John Macpherson, had been invited to perform the opening ceremony. He and Lady Macpherson travelled up from Lagos in their special white train, to which Bryan's coaches were attached at Kaduna junction. Angela and I were not able to join the party until the following day and the plan was that we should drive up, early, by car. Unfortunately, another of those violent and prolonged tornadoes swept the country during the night and the rain was so torrential that the road was reduced to a sea of slippery mud wherever it had not been tarred. Bryan telephoned me from Zaria to stay at home unless conditions improved. However, by eight o'clock that morning, the rain had stopped and, not wanting to miss such an important occasion, I decided to chance it. On the way, we passed cars and lorries abandoned in the quagmire at rakish angles and giant trees lying prostrate, their roots exposed. Several had fallen across the road and occasionally we had to wait while workmen moved them. All too often we almost shuddered to a standstill in the soft clay and it was only thanks to Audu-Mai-Kano's skilful driving that we at last arrived at Zaria. Of course, we were late. Sardauna, in his horn-rimmed spectacles, was already giving the address, as we entered the hall and we stood for a few minutes behind the great crowd of Nigerians which occupied the room. As we normally sat close to Sardauna on such occasions, this was the first time I had felt, as a member of the crowd, the impact of his personality. He was a big man in every sense of the word, tall and heavily-built for a man so fond of games. Though nearly fifty, he still played fives whenever he had the time and, in Sokoto days, we had often watched him energetically playing cricket. Sardauna's face often reminded me, though in shape only, of a Tudor king. From a high-domed forehead the face was broad all the way down to the neck. His chin was fringed with a curly beard, though the long, upper lip and the rest of his face were clean-shaven. There was in his expression a combination of humour, serenity and warmth. Though his speech was smooth and unexcited and he used rather long English words, he had the knack of developing an intimate relationship with his audience and of making them laugh. The younger generation especially adored him. His love of expensive clothes and scents, large cars and bodies of retainers was something which they understood and approved.

The time soon came for the Macphersons to leave Nigeria. Everyone was sad to say 'Farewell' to this graceful and friendly pair who had done so much for the country during their period of office. After an interval, we heard that Sir James Robertson, who had served many years in the Sudan, was to succeed as Governor General and would shortly be in the North on his first visit. When he arrived, Northern leaders were delighted to be addressed by him in Arabic, even though only a few were fluent in the language. They felt sure that one who had lived so long in a Muslim country would understand their problems. This was important to them, for although he was likely to make frequent tours, he would be based in Lagos and would have to spend much of his time there. Lagos had always been isolated from the rest of Nigeria and absorbed in its own, sophisticated existence. Of the thousands of white people who were stationed there, a few knew the North but many never travelled far inland. If they thought about the region at all, it was merely to dismiss it as a land of feudal princes and stuffy British officers. 'Dirt and Dignity' was the slogan used to sum up the North.

By this time, Lagos was beginning to change its attitude since the leading Federal minister was a Northerner and so, too, were many of his colleagues.

Nigeria was now entering the last and most difficult stage of her journey to independence. Britain was still responsible for the territory but by now all except the most senior British officials were working under Nigerians. Most of them doggedly adapted themselves to the new regime and the few who could not do so retired. Perhaps the departmental directors had the bitterest pill to swallow. After years of conscientious toil, these men had reached the top rung only to find it occupied by a Nigerian minister. A few years later, even the title of 'Director' was abolished in favour of the word 'Adviser'. However, the professional men, i.e. the doctors, engineers and so on, serving under them remained about 90 per cent British, since there were still so few Northern Nigerians qualified for such posts.

But the directors were not the only ones to find the new Nigeria unsettling. The chiefs had taken the many and great changes so far with considerable calm, but they now began to be seriously alarmed at the growing influence of young and inexperienced politicians who had begun to stir up trouble between Muslims and non-Muslims and to interfere with the local courts and in other matters that were not their concern. The chiefs felt that their own prestige was being undermined to the extent that they could no longer carry out their duties. The politicians, for their part, were struggling ostentatiously to assert themselves in the eyes of the peasantry who, so it seemed to them, still obstinately looked to the chiefs for guidance. Friction between the chiefs and the ministers was inevitable and there were two weeks of tension, highly charged with emotion, when a major explosion seemed imminent.

Eventually a meeting of reconciliation between the two parties was arranged. Unfortunately, Sardauna and his ministers wanted to fix matters so that open criticism would be stifled from the start. Bryan, who was ultimately responsible, knew that this would merely drive the trouble underground and would not agree.

Sardauna became angry and, when Bryan had to leave on a tour for Kano, relations were highly strained. During his absence, Abubakar came up from Lagos and succeeded in persuading Sardauna that Bryan was trying to hold the region together, not split it apart as some of his, Sardauna's followers were doing. When Bryan returned, Abubakar came to see him. 'You must,' he insisted, 'restore your old relationship with Sardauna. You should see him or keep in touch by telephone every day if possible, just as you used to do. He will be asking to see you later in the morning.'

When Sardauna came to Government House, a highly-charged scene developed to which I was an unintending witness, when I walked into the drawing room to greet him, as was customary. Sardauna had been deeply affected by the first serious rift that he and Bryan had had and I found him in a state of some emotion as he admitted that he had been at fault and asked that the old friendly relationship should be restored.

As far as the women were concerned, some headway had been made in their education. A flourishing girls' secondary school and a teacher training college had been established at Kano while another secondary school for girls had just been opened at Ilorin, 300 miles south of Kaduna. This was a large, modern building, expensively equipped. Some people thought it grossly extravagant, but Dr Geary the Director for Education for women was determined and she had insisted on nothing but the best.

Socially, progress with the women was slower. Prominent Northern males were not really impressed when told that Muslims in up-to-date countries like Pakistan had ceased locking up their wives. Perhaps the presence in their midst of so many emancipated white women merely confirmed them in their attitude. They had no wish to see their wives assert themselves and go about so disgracefully underdressed. British women, in the briefest of shorts and scantiest tops, could be seen in the hot weather pushing prams round Kaduna or shopping in the canteens and although this was a common sight, it was none the less painful to strict Muslims.

The European women were, in the main, not deeply interested in much outside their own families and circles of friends. No doubt, many of them would really have liked to make friends with

Northern Nigerian women and to help them, but there was little they could do which would not have been resented.

However, a growing group of educated young Northerners, whose horizons had been widened by courses of study in Britain, were keen that their wives should play a more sophisticated role in public life, though, in the face of strong disapproval of the older chiefs, only a handful had the courage to put such theories into practice.

At the Annual General Meeting of the Red Cross, one rather argumentative male member of this group stood up and asked me why there were no Northern women to serve on this committee. I replied, 'Good, I am glad that you want Northern women to serve on this committee. This is what I have always wanted too. I suggest we start by inviting some of your wives.' But they thought I had put the questioner very neatly in his place and my serious response was greeted by guffaws of admiring laughter.

A few years before, a society for the wives of colonial civil servants had opened in London with branches in all the dependent territories. It was called the Women's Corona Society. Members of the branch in Kaduna held coffee mornings and other functions in different members houses and periodically we had a large tea party at Government House. The Christian wives of ministers and of other Nigerian government officials usually came and so did a few of the Muslim ones. One of these was Aishetu, the Makama of Bida's young and charming wife, for the Minister of Education was enlightened. Another was Ina Talib, the slim and graceful wife of a Northern official in the Finance Ministry. She was also a teacher at the Capital School and 'Brown Owl' of a Brownie Pack, which met at Makama's house and catered for the daughters of the ministers.

Each time we held a garden party for the Women's Corona Society we hoped that the Premier's wives would come, but we were so often disappointed that eventually the secretary asked if she should continue to invite them. Fortunately, we agreed that she should, for one day, to our surprise and delight, we saw one of the Sardauna's cars advancing up the drive in the procession of those conveying guests to the front porch. In due course, three of the Sardauna's wives alighted, most friendly and talkative and full of the Fulani repartee and the Sokoto charm with which we were so familiar in their menfolk.

One day, the Red Cross field officer came to see me. She told me that the Reverend Mother of the Kaduna Convent was worried about one of her teachers. This girl's husband, Ali Akilu, had gone to London for a four-year degree course at University College. Since he left, she had given birth to twin boys, but both babies had died and she was lonely and depressed. Reverend Mother wanted to help the girl, whose name was Caroline, to join her husband. She had heard that the Red Cross was looking for a Northerner to train as a field officer in the UK and she believed Caroline might be suitable. When I met the girl, I thought so too. Ali Akilu, as a university graduate, was likely to become one of the leading men in the North, so Caroline would be admirably placed for such a job. She was a sensitive, co-operative person with experience of leadership as a teacher and in the Guide movement. She would need greater forcefulness of character than she seemed at the time to possess but this was quite likely to develop with age and experience.

Unfortunately, the Northern Regional Scholarship Board, which was paying all Ali's expenses, could not afford to do the same for student's wives. It seemed that Caroline's scholastic achievements, though enough to qualify for teaching, were too modest to entitle her to an overseas scholarship in her own right. Nor had the Regional Red Cross sufficient funds for such a purpose, even though the whole future of the Society in the North depended on training local men and women to take over posts then held by Europeans. Indeed, London Headquarters had sent us field officers on the strict understanding that they should hand over to Northern Nigerians within four years.

The position was explained to the ministers who, as usual, were quick to see the value of the scheme. At once they began to think of ways and means of financing it and six months later Caroline sailed for England. After a course at Barnett Hill, the Red Cross Training Centre, she was attached to the Westminster Branch of the Red Cross where one of her duties was to help take 'Meals on Wheels' to the elderly and infirm and she loved this.

Ali and Caroline had been allocated furnished rooms with a gas ring in Notting Hill. At first she found shopping perplexing because so few of the foods to which she was accustomed were available. 'I've tried *everywhere* to find yams', she told me in desperation when I met her for lunch in London during leave. She and Ali had been living mainly on such foods as breakfast cereals and tinned fish. I tried to make some helpful suggestions. Caroline had seen most of the sights of London but she had not visited the National Gallery so we spent a plesant hour there. For me, the pleasure was in watching her face and listening to her delighted comments. The modern pictures were in a style familiar enough, but the Gainsboroughs and Constables were a revelation and so too were the early Italian pictures and she was amazed at the age of them. But I had to hurry her past the picture of the martyrdom of Saint Sebastian, because this display of human cruelty distressed her so much.

15 PROGRESS, PARTIES AND POLITICS

Soon after returning to Nigeria, we left Kaduna for the Residents' Conference which was held that year once more at Jos. Instead of puffing slowly upwards to the Plateau by train, we now flew in an Auster, a four-seater, single-engined aircraft, whose cruising speed was ninety miles an hour. It was rather like rising into the air in a sports car with wings. We usually flew fairly low, at about three thousand feet, and this gave us a leisurely view of what lay below. Indeed, unless we tactfully averted our gaze during take off or landing, we had an all too intimate glimpse of the insides of the compounds.

Leaving the capital and its suburbs, we crossed the Kaduna River and were soon passing over featureless woodland. On rare occasions, the monotony was broken by a village which seen from above looked like a network of walled cells in which tiny round roofs were neatly spaced. Furrowed farms radiated outwards and here and there, isolated locust bean trees cast black pools of shade. After about half an hour of level flight, rocky outcrops began to appear and as these humps grew larger and more frequent, we began to gain height. A sudden chill struck the Auster and we reached in the racks for our jackets. Soon we crossed the edge of the escarpment and were flying over the treeless tracts of the Plateau. Roads, like ribbons, ran through undulating valleys and wound their way over craggy hills.

In some places, pagan villages clustered amongst the rocks, their terraced farms enclosed in hedges of prickly cactus. Several times we flew over a tin mine where bulldozers like gigantic yellow dung beetles, pushed the soil, and excavators bit into cliffs of clay. Nearby, in tidy rows, were the miners' cottages and, further away, the homes and well stocked gardens of a mines manager and his European staff.

Flying into Jos was, as usual, a bumpy business. As our flaps went down and we started to lose height, we were roughly jerked down and thrust up by pockets of Plateau air. However, at last we were safely on the ground and driving the two miles to Tudun Wada, the Governor's hill-station retreat. This was a thatched bungalow set close to the top of the hill. Behind it were huge rocks in which lived a family of grey monkeys. They varied in numbers but usually there were an adult male with two females and two or three young. This time, we were intrigued to find that since our last visit, one of the females had just had a baby. It clung to her chest, facing her, and thus rode astride her hips as she leapt from rock to rock.

In front, the house looked down a terraced slope into a valley full of trees through which blue hills about three miles away could just be glimpsed. Flamboyants and bougainvillaea bloomed on the lower terrace in fiery scarlet and purple. The bungalow had gables at either side, enclosing on three sides a paved patio. The house opened onto the patio through a latticed porch in the centre. It was lined with cushioned benches and we used to sit there, in the cool of the evening, drinking in the view, soothed by the scent of orange blossoms from two citrus trees in tubs.

The African town of Jos was sprawling and cosmopolitan. It had a long trading quarter which led to a vast *sabon gari*. The 'station', which was still largely European, ranged round a golf course between the town and Tudun Wada hill. Tucked between the trees and built, in many cases, of local stone, the houses blended attractively with the scenery. The largest of these was a government-run hotel, called 'Hill Station', a long thatched bungalow which ran along the crest of the hill about two hundred yards from our house. The guests were either accommodated in the main building or in one of the seven chalets which were dotted about in the grounds. At this time, the whole of 'Hill Station' was taken over for the Residents' Conference.

The local potentate was a large and genial man named Rwang Pam, Chief of the Birom tribe. He dressed like a Muslim emir with a turban and gown, though in fact he was a Christian. His wife accompanied him on all but the most formal occasions. She was generously built, too, and smiled a great deal though she was more silent than her husband. Some of the Birom were educated Christians, like their chief, though, unlike him, they tended to wear the European-type of clothes. The uneducated ones were still pagan and lived almost in a state of nature. The women shaved their heads and smoked pipes and were able to carry heavy loads on their heads. They wore bunches of freshly gathered leaves in the usual strategic positions. The men had flaps of leather which hung from the waist. It was said that the Plateau pagans owed their robust physique to the strong beer which they brewed from local corn. They certainly drank deeply whenever there was cause for celebration. On these occasions the sound of drumming and pagan merriment would ring out at night across the valleys from the hill top hamlets.

Civilisation was, however, rapidly gaining ground with these simple people. Not only the missions but also the Lagos politicians were preaching that nudity was shameful. So, many of the women began to wrap themselves, leaves included, in lengths of homespun cloth.

The Residents' Conference lasted a week but we only stayed in Jos for the first few days. It was Bryan's custom to open proceedings and then let the Residents continue it themselves. We managed to fit in a cocktail party for all the members and their wives and to have individual Residents over to Tudun Wada for a talk and drink before lunch or dinner. The wives came for morning coffee while their husbands were busy at the conference and I much enjoyed meeting so many old friends, for I had known most of them years ago when we were all newer to the country.

Unfortunately, we were seldom able to visit Jos but two or three years running managed to spend Christmas there, when we were joined by Michael and Geoffrey for the school holidays. The cottage atmosphere was perfect for this kind of family reunion and there was no need for the large scale official entertaining which would have been unavoidable at Kaduna. We had many visitors though, and these included the Resident and his wife, Rex and Dorothy Niven, and members of the prosperous mining community. They, in their turn, were most hospitable to us. The Plateau had an independence of outlook which we found refreshing after the more conventional Kaduna.

There was plenty to amuse our children, a pantomime, given by a local dramatic society, a miniature railway which operated on Boxing Day, sailing on a large dam belonging to one of the mining firms and swimming and sunbathing at their Club pool. For the boys it was sheer bliss to shed their winter school clothes and put on bathing trunks and sun glasses, though caution was needed for this sudden change could be perilous to white English skins.

On Christmas morning there was a massive gathering at the Church of St Piran, the patron saint of tin miners. This was a simple white-washed building with a corrugated iron roof set amongst willowy trees. Inside it was furnished with thick blue carpets and locally carved mahogany and so gaily decorated with flowers that it was hard to believe that we were celebrating Christmas and not Whitsun. Carols were sung enthusiastically by a mixed adult choir which half-faced the congregation. St Piran's was nominally Church of England but welcomed people of many other denominations.

As soon as we returned to Kaduna, Bryan was plunged once more into the problems of politics. There were three major parties in the North at this time. The largest and most influential was the Northern Peoples' Congress, usually known as the NPC. At first, this party had been supported by the emirs and most of its leaders came from the traditional ruling class. This was the main reason for its popularity. The people liked to be led by those they knew and trusted. Unfortunately, as the NPC grew large, it attracted a small fringe of young extremists. The emirs disapproved of what they considered to be wild behaviour, from no matter what quarter. When they heard of the activities of these young men they became much less enthusiastic and eventually they moved out of party politics altogether.

Nevertheless, led by the charismatic Sardauna and the scholarly Abubakar Tafawa Balewa, the party had won a resounding victory at the last federal and regional elections.

Of the two main opposition parties, the older was the Northern Elements Progressive Union, NEPU. This included a number of disgruntled NA officials, unruly elements of the Hausa trading community and the riff-raff of the towns. NEPU indiscriminately opposed all established authority, both African and European. It was this party's newspaper, the *Comet*, which had attacked Dr Smith at the time of the *El Duniya* disaster at Kano. NEPU had formed an alliance with the NCNC (National Council for Nigeria and the Cameroons), the largest of the two main parties in the South who regarded NEPU as a useful chink in the Northern armour. It was also supported by certain left-wingers in the United Kingdom, who were impressed by NEPU's talk of democracy and believed that they ought to encourage the rebellious 'under dog' of the North.

The other opposition party in the North was the United Middle Belt Congress, the UMBC, which drew its members from the non-Muslim minority. It was called 'Middle Belt' because most of its adherents came from the central zone of Nigeria. All were of pagan origin though a sizable proportion had been educated at mission schools and converted to Christianity. Up to the time of the British occupation, fifty years earlier, these people had lived in terror of the slave-raiding gangs of the Muslim emirs. Though the Middle Belt people were loyal to the British, they were not pleased when most of the Ministers first appointed came from the Muslim ruling families from further North. Independence was swiftly approaching and they did not relish being governed by the descendants of their one-time oppressors. There had been no other choice at the time, for, in a largely illiterate clountry, men like Sardauna and Makama alone had both the education and experience in administration that was needed for the task. The Muslim leaders, in the past, regarded the Middle Belt people contemptuously as ignorant and uncivilised, but they were now forced to change their views. In recent years, Mission schools had multiplied and had found enthusiastic pupils. In fact, progress in education was so rapid that some were beginning to outstrip the more conservative Muslims from further North. The Ministers could no longer ignore the danger to the unity of the North of a disgruntled Middle Belt. UMBC leaders were already demanding a separate Middle Belt Region. In this they were supported by the Ibos and Yorubas of the South, who welcomed the prospect of a split in the North since it was much larger than both their regions put together.

Sardauna and his fellow ministers now realised that they must include a fair proportion of Middle Belt non-Muslims in the 'cabinet', and once this decision was put into effect, they quickly began to feel respect for their new Christian colleagues. Peter Achimuga had been the first of these, then came Pastor David Lot, a Baptist minister from the Plateau and the Roman Catholic, George Ohikere, from Kabba.

Unfortunately, not all differences were settled so peacefully. In 1955, minor outbreaks of violence in places like Kano and Gusau were becoming unpleasantly frequent. The main culprits were the extremist gangs of NEPU and the NPC. But the most serious conflict of all had taken place in Kano two years earlier between Northerners and Southerners. During three days of rioting, thirty-six people had been killed and nearly two hundred severely injured. The trouble began at Lagos during a meeting of the House of Representatives. Southern politicians were pressing the British government to grant 'self-government in 1956'. The Northern leaders thought that neither side was likely to be ready as soon as this. In any case, their own people lagged so far behind the rest of Nigeria, educationally, that if independence came too soon, the North might well be dominated for all time by the South. The Northerners therefore refused to give the motion their support. The Southern politicians were scornful and bent on revenge. In consequence, the Northern members of the House of Representatives, who then included three chiefs, were mocked and jeered at by Southern hooligans whenever they set foot outside their lodgings in Lagos and at railway stations where their train stopped on its North-bound journey. Northerners were normally tolerant and slow to anger, but such insults to their leaders were more than they could endure. While they were still boiling with rage at these events, one of the Southern political parties, the Action Group, decided to tour the North in the hope of attracting Northern adherents. They could scarcely have chosen a more inopportune moment. The very day they reached Kano, rioting broke out between Northerners and Southerners, nearly all of whom were Ibo. The ordinary Yoruba got on quite well with the Hausa, for many were Muslim. But between the Hausa and the more headstrong Ibo there had always been dislike and now was a time to pay off old scores. The other main Southern party, the NCNC, not wanting to be left out, had, meantime decided that they too must make a political tour of the North and were on their way to Kaduna. However, a message was delivered to their train telling them how serious the situation was in Kano and they wisely decided to return to Lagos. It was three days and three nights before the Northern anger was assuaged and the casualties might have been ten times as great but for the skill, courage and forbearance of the police.

16 THE QUEEN'S VISIT AND THE ROYAL DURBAR

Towards the end of 1955, there came a momentous announcement which caused all differences to be temporarily forgotten. This was the news that Her Majesty the Queen and HRH the Duke of Edinburgh would be making an official tour of Nigeria in the February of the following year. Although the former Prince of Wales, later the Duke of Windsor, had toured the country thirty years earlier, no reigning monarch had ever set foot on Nigerian soil. The excitement was tremendous. Some of the emirs and other leading men had already been presented to the Queen during visits to the United Kingdom. All had feelings of intense loyalty towards her. Portraits of the Royal family hung in every emir's palace and were amongst their most treasured possessions.

The tour was to last three weeks, of which six days would be spent in the Northern Region. The Royal guests would be in Kaduna for three days, staying with us at Government House. They would go to Jos for a weekend's rest at Tudun Wada. The last day of the tour was to be spent in Kano *en route* by air for home.

I was on leave when the news reached me. Once I had recovered from the shock and excitement, I began to think of the domestic problems involved. John the Cook and his two assistants were efficient by local standards, but the tasks ahead would obviously be beyond their unaided capabilities.

By a stroke of luck, Denys Woodward, the chairman of Nigerian Hotels, was a great friend who happened to live at Hythe. Whilst on leave, we told him of our problem and he at once offered to help. The result was that catering experts from Nigeria Hotels took over the supervision of Government House kitchen and dining room for the duration of the Royal visit, using our own domestic staff. I was more than thankful to be relieved of this responsibility and the arrangement proved to be an outstanding success. All that I had to do, in advance of the visit, was to consider the caterers' detailed suggestions and to work out the menus.

Despite all that had been done at Government House while we had been there, much refurnishing and re-equipment was needed to make it suitable for entertaining royalty. The Queen had especially asked that there be no undue expense in connection with her visit. The ministers, on the other hand, were determined that Northern Nigeria should put on a truly stupendous show, no matter what the cost. So my problem was to please them and at the same time obey the Queen's instructions. I did my best to strike some kind of happy medium.

Owing to the children's school holidays, I was unable to return to Nigeria until just a month before the Queen was expected, Bryan having preceded me by several weeks. I found Government House in a state of indescribable chaos. During my absence, a representative from Nigeria Hotels had inspected the kitchen and had demanded structural alterations and much new equipment. Holes had been hacked through the walls in several places for new electric cables, leaving piles of rubble and white dust everywhere. A few days later, a mammoth refrigerator was laboriously pushed in by ten strong men, five each side. Three of them could have stood comfortably side by side inside it. All the plaster had been stripped from the walls of the Royal bedrooms (normally ours) and the whole place was festooned with wires and choking with powdered cement. The loose covers, carpets and curtains, which I had ordered in England, had still not arrived, neither had the new bathroom suite.

Not only Government House but all over Kaduna there was frenzied activity with nothing near completion. Yet there was no panic. On the contrary, those concerned were cheerful and optimistic. 'Of course we shall be ready in time,' they all said, 'even if we have to work all night.' And this is exactly what many of them did towards the end.

One of the major operations was the conversion of the race course into a giant stadium for the durbar. Two long grandstands were under construction and experts from the Ministry of Agriculture were trying to grow grass on the hard-baked earth of the arena, a thankless task in the height of the dry season. An independent water supply for the grass had been set up, with an elaborate system of sprinklers. But for this, it was feared that our Royal guests would not be able to see the show for clouds of dust.

Every chief of the region was invited to attend the durbar with a fixed quota of followers. By Christmas, thousands of horses and men had already set off on their long journey to the capital; some

came from over 400 miles away. All had to be provided with food
and shelter, both on the route and in Kaduna. For this purpose, a
vast camp had been prepared in the capital. It covered two hills
and a broad valley between. Row upon neat row of grass huts had
been erected, with horse lines, first aid posts, fire fighting stations,
veterinary clinics for sick horses, newspaper kiosks, markets and
electric stree lighting. Each cross road in the camp was sign posted
to direct the visitors to the areas set aside for each contingent and
loud speakers were set up at intervals so that verbal instructions
could be given at vital moments. Behind the huts, trenches were
dug for sanitary purposes. Unfortunately, simple people, living
near Kaduna, did not understand this and the rumour spread that
the pits were for the disposal of the dead. It was lucky that this
tale did not reach beyond Zaria, fifty-five miles away, so not many
were deterred from coming. Traditional enemies were indeed
living side by side in the camp but they were too pre-occupied with
the part each one was to play in the durbar to concern themselves
with tribal feuds.

Schoolboys and girls were also on their way to Kaduna from all
over the North, for their show would be on the third day of the
visit. Kaduna schools were to provide all the accommodation by
converting class rooms into temporary dormitories and having
army huts erected in the grounds.

A week before the Queen's arrival, preparations had reached
fever heat. Already several contingents had arrived and were
living in the camp. There was much blowing of horns and shuffling
of hooves. At Government House, the Royal bedrooms were still
not ready. The tiling in the Duke of Edinburgh's bathroom had not
come up to the exacting standards of the Ministry of Works officials
in charge and they pulled it udone and were re-doing the job
themselves, working late into each night. My curtains, carpets and
furniture had at last arrived, but the Indian rugs were covered with
loose pile so they had to be spread out on the lawns each morning
to be brushed, then taken indoors and hoovered.

The grass on the durbar ground was beginning to show. In the
centre, between the two grandstands, a specious Royal dais had
been erected and painted white and blue. There was a Royal crest
on top and at the sides there were window boxes later to be filled
with scarlet geraniums. In the streets, triumphal archways,
decorative shields and groups of flags and banners were being
hoisted into position to mark the Royal routes. Then came repeated
and painstaking rehearsals, not only of the Durbar, but of every

ceremony, no matter how small, so that every soldier, policeman, civilian and every driver of an official car knew exactly what to do and when.

At last the day came. Bryan and I were at the airport to meet the Royal visitors with the Premier, the Chief Justice, the principal chiefs, the ministers, the Brigadier and top-ranking officials. Across the tarmac, a military guard of honour waited; tough Nigerians in scarlet jackets, khaki shorts, red fez cap with gold tassels, standing at ease in two solid rows. At the far end was the regional mascot, a ground hornbill. This was a black bird the size of a turkey, with a long curved beak and wicked, beady eyes. She stood patiently in the sun, pecking the ground, beside a soldier to whom she was attached by her collar and lead. Meanwhile, another soldier with a yellow duster went from man to man, flicking off the last specks of dust from highly polished boots. Then, suddenly, all eyes were turned skywards as a faint buzz announced the approach of the Royal aircraft. She touched down and taxied into position at the other end of the red carpet, brilliant silver in the strong morning light. The gangway was wheeled up, the door opened and there was the Queen, smiling. She stepped lightly down with the Duke of Edinburgh just behind her. After shaking hands, Bryan's bow, my much-practiced curtsey and the presentations, we all stood to attention for the National Anthem. Then the Queen and the Duke of Edinburgh inspected the Guard of Honour. When Prince Philip reached the ground hornbill, he and the bird stood for quite a second or two, eyeing one another.

After a fly-past of Canberra jets of the Royal Air Force, the Royal party drove slowly in an open Rolls Royce to Government House, two miles away. The route was gaily decorated all the way and lined with horsemen and people on foot, all in their Durbar outfits, waving swords and cheering.

We thought that the Queen might be too tired, after her journey, for any further events that day other than the State Dinner that night, though provisional arrangements had been made for her to watch a polo match after tea, if she so wished. Not only did she do this but, when Bryan told her about the durbar camp, she said that she would like to see that too. So that the visit should be informal and free from outside intruders, only half an hour's warning was deliberately given. When the Queen arrived at the gateway to the camp, the news that she had come flashed round and she was given a tumultuous welcome. The people were really quite beside themselves with joy and the police, who had also had only half an hour's warning, had some difficulty in controlling them. At one point, the crowd was so dense that the Royal car over-ran the traffic police at the place where it should have turned and came to a dead end. Bryan, who was acting as guide, had visions of going down in history as the Governor who lost his Queen. Keeping calm, he directed the driver along a rough track between the camp sites of two contingents and to his relief managed to rejoin the main camp road and the rest of the procession which had been completely cut off. The Queen and Prince Philip were quite unperturbed and shortly afterwards they left the car and walked almost unescorted through the crowd and onto a small hill from which the whole camp could be viewed.

The next day was Durbar Day. As the show was to take place in the morning, the Queen was to have worn day clothes. However, the chiefs begged Bryan to ask her to appear in a long evening gown and a tiara. When the Queen heard this she at once agreed, although, as she said to me that morning, it did seem strange to be going about in evening clothes at ten in the morning.

The magnificence of the Durbar exceeded everyone's expectations. Each chief rode proudly at the head of his contingent, accompanied by one or two servants on foot who held a huge, fringed umbrella, twirling it all the time. Sword bearers preceded him and, following, were row upon row of proud horsemen, some in plumed helmets and chain mail, others in the highest and stiffest turbans and the most elaborate gowns in beautifully-blended colours. The horses were richly dressed too, with jingling ornaments, decorated saddles and quilted armour. Those from Bornu even wore trousers. The Middle Belt contingents included teams of tribal dancers, mostly male, some in masks and grass skirts, others naked except for loin cloths and beaded anklets, their supple bodies stained red and oiled. They jived, turning and twisting and springing up into the air to the rhythm of drums and pipes. There were parties of jugglers and tumblers and occasionally a solitary acrobat, turning somersaults and cartwheels, walking on his hands and generally making everyone laugh. Most stupendous of all was the *Jahi* at the end. This was a charge of horsemen, brandishing spears, a customary salute to a great ruler. About sixty horsemen assembled in a line about fifty yards from the Royal pavilion. At a given moment, with their weapons held aloft, they galloped forward, racing one another to the Royal dais and pulling up only just in time. Then they waved their spears fiercely at the Queen and plunged them into the ground. One rider, well over seventy, broke his girth strap during the charge and fell off, but he managed to pick himself up again, apparently unhurt. Altogether, more than six thousand people had paid homage to the Queen.

When it was ended, Prince Philip leaned over and said to her, 'You know, we shall never see anything like this again.'

Then, in dead silence, the Queen rose to speak. With a clear voice she told these, her people, how closely she watched their progress and cared for their traditions.

As the Royal guests drove slowly out of the arena and the cheers died away, this most colourful and romantic of spectacles had come to a close.

That afternoon, the Royal Garden Party took place in the grounds of Government House, attended by a thousand people, most of whom were Nigerian. As they circulated on the terraced lawns, the band of the Nigeria Regiment played light music. The Queen, accompanied by Bryan and her Standard Bearer, made her way between the guests, stopping at pre-arranged intervals for presentations and friendly talks. Meanwhile, I was doing my best to perform a similar duty for Prince Philip. He chatted to many not on the list, much to their delight, hailing them with a friendly, 'Who are you? What's your job?'

The party ended with an investiture. The first to receive an honour was the much loved Sultan of Sokoto, the 'Commander of the Faithful', who received the accolade of Knighthood, an honour awarded to him some years previously. Then came thirty six others, both Nigerian and British. They included the first Northern Nigerian woman ever to receive an honour from the Queen. She was Kubura, a school teacher from Birnin Kebbi and, by a strange chance, the mother of the baby I had seen all those years ago at the Sokoto Girls' Training Centre.

The next day was the Children's Day. Their show was also held on the Durbar Ground. This time, the Guard of Honour was formed by the Boy's Company of the Nigeria Regiment. No adults could have been smarter or prouder than these young soldiers. Forming a huge horse shoe, were contingents of children from all the twelve provinces in the region, each section being marked by a banner. There were also representatives of the boy scouts, girl guides, boys and girls brigades, Red Cross cadets and of the other youth organisations. The Queen and the Duke of Edinburgh began by driving round this vast assembly in a Land Rover, while the children waved their flags and cheered. Then they returned to the centre of the arena where a typical Northern Nigerian village in miniature had been set up. There were the familiar groups of round mud huts, with cone-shaped roofs, surrounded by corn-stalk fences but the huts were only five feet high. The villagers were schoolchildren, dressed in grown-up clothes. The girls were cooking, drawing water from a well, weaving on hand looms, spinning thread from lumps of cotton wool, decorating calabashes with poker work patterns and grinding and pounding corn. Some of the boys were busy at the blacksmith's forge, others were weaving mats and dying cloth while a group, just outside the village, were energetically hoeing a patch of farmland. In the middle, some girls were merrily performing a folk dance in the course of which one girl was tossed high into the air.

What really brought the house down was a boy with a donkey. He was trying to make it carry both himself and a light, but bulky, load of cornstalks. The animal obstinately refused to move forward and kept kicking and bucking. The boy held on for several minutes but in the end both he and his load came off with a thump.

The Queen and Prince Philip walked around the village with Sardauna, Makaman Bida, the Education Minister, and Tony Shillingford, the European Director of Education. Our Royal guests asked so many questions and were so fascinated by the display that they overstayed the scheduled time by half an hour.

The next item on the Royal programme was a visit to the Sleeping Sickness Research Centre, where the Queen and Prince Philip were shown the latest methods of fighting this disease and of controlling the tsetse flies which carry it. Just outside the centre, a model Fulani settlement had been set up where Sardauna and Peter Achimugu, the minister responsible, with veterinary experts explained how the nomad communities lived and managed their herds and flocks. The Fulani women were thrilled to see the Queen so closely and proudly showed her and Prince Philip their babies as well as their cattle.

Before the Royal visit, the police had urged Bryan to have the grounds of Government House surrounded with coils of barbed wire, three layers deep. Nothing else would give adequate protection, they felt, for there was no wall along the boundary, only a scanty wire fence. Bryan felt that the barbed wire would make the place look like a concentration camp, so he had a better idea. He asked the great chiefs to lend members of their personal bodyguards, to form a mobile guard which would patrol Government House boundary night and day. When the emirs were approached, they agree delightedly. Several times, the Queen and Prince Philip noticed these fierce warriors on horseback, pacing along outside the fence, in their chain mail and plumed helmets and armed with spears which they were plainly prepared to use on any intruder. One afternoon, the Queen talked with several of them and took photographs with her ciné camera.

The last event in Kaduna was a State Visit to the Lugard Hall. Bryan, as President of the House of Chiefs, had to be at the Hall to greet the Royal guests when they arrived. With him was Rex Niven, who was President of the House of Assembly. While we waited in the shade of the bougainvillaea which grew over the main porch to the Lugard Hall, the Queen and Prince Philip were approaching in the open Rolls Royce in a stately procession of cars. The Queen was wearing a gold embroidered evening gown, a magnificent tiara and the Order of the Garter. The Duke of Edinburgh was in the uniform of an Admiral of the Fleet and he also wore the Order of the Garter. Unfortunately, as the motorcade approached the avenue of mahoganies leading up to the Hall, the Rolls Royce engine became overheated and stalled. The crowd, characteristically helpful and uninhibited, stopped waving and at once began to push the Royal car. As soon as it was once more in motion, the engine started up and the procession continued as before.

As the party made its way into the Chamber, spot lights were switched onto the Queen and the Duke of Edinburgh and the Queen's diamonds flashed and sparkled continuously.

Facing the throne in the horse shoe shaped tiers of the Hall were sitting in great splendour the Chiefs and the Members of the House of Assembly. Sardauna, the Premier, alone wore a simple white gown and roped headdress of a pilgrim from Mecca.

The ceremony opened with the reading of the Loyal Address by the Premier, which expressed the Region's devotion to the Queen and the Commonwealth and its pleasure at the Royal visit. The Queen then replied, thanking the Premier and expressing her and her husband's deep interest in Northern Nigeria and its progress towards self-government. She mentioned appreciatively the work of the British Civil Servants and the Missionaries.

After dinner that evening, there was a display of tribal dancing on the lawns of Government House. The first team danced a mime, representing good, evil, a corn harvest and the killing of a leopard. Drummers kept up a staccato rhythm and a piper played a haunting little ditty. The second team danced on stilts, wearing white pointed hoods which totally concealed their faces. The third troup were those muscular men of the durbar whose bodies were stained dark red and oiled. They wore scarlet caps and rattling anklets and their dance consisted of rapid vigorous movements and leaps int the air. The last team were, by tradition, warriors. Their dance represented flights of bees and locusts. They were accompanied by a solo singer and a band of drums, whistles and horns. When the display was over, the four teams returned to their quarters in the Durbar Camp three miles away, dancing, drumming and singing as they went.

The following morning, the Royal party left Kaduna by air for their brief weekend's rest at Jos. Tudun Wada had been redecorated and refurnished and new bathrooms and a new kitchen had been added. I feared that the noise the workmen had made might have frightened away the family of monkeys who lived in the boulders behind the bungalow. However, they were hiding and during the peace of that weekend, they came out to play so that our guests not only saw them but took photographs as well.

Soon after their arrival at Jos airport, Prince Philip was taken to see a tin mine. For the Queen, the only public engagement was attendance at Morning Service at St Piran's Church on the Sunday.

Early the following day, our guests left by air for the Eastern Region, stopping for a brief half hour's visit to Makurdi, in the Northern Region on the way.

When the Queen and the Duke of Edinburgh had completed their tour of the other two Regions and of Lagos, they stopped for a day at Kano on their way back to London by air. The walled city was lavishly decorated for the occasion and the Emir had assembled even more horsemen than had attended the durbar. The Royal tour of the city concluded with a visit to the Emir's Palace.

The Royal guests passed beneath the towered entrance into a courtyard which was ornamented with flags and banners. Here the Emir welcomed them and conducted them into his council chamber. Once the formalities were ended, the Queen visited the women's part of the palace, and spoke to the Emir's four wives. It was not possible for any of the men to accompany her except the Emir himself, so it was my task to act as interpreter. She visited the rooms of each of the wives in turn, beginning with that of the Uwargida. On the way we passed through a series of dark passages, courtyards and lofty mud-built halls, some of which the Emir told us were over three hundred years old. Indeed, the whole atmosphere was so medieval that the Queen was astonished to see a large and up-to-date refrigerator standing in one of the corridors. By the time we rejoined the men we found that they were beginning to wonder what had happened as we had been away much longer than they had expected.

At last, after nightfall, we all went to the airport to say 'Goodbye' to our Royal guests. As we watched their aircraft, ablaze with lights, vanish into the night sky, a feeling of loneliness and sadness came over us that this wonderful experience had ended.

17 FAREWELLS

As soon as we had recovered from the excitement of the Royal visit, preparations began for the marriage of Sarah to Victor Hibbs, who had been Bryan's ADC when she had been out with us. Government House was an ideal setting for such an occasion and though there were no longer professional caterers or florists actually in Kaduna, there were plenty of willing helpers from amongst our friends. One had been trained in flower arrangement by Constance Spry. The icing of the three tier wedding cake, which I had made, was carried out by a sergeant of the Army Catering Corps who arrived at Government House on a motor bicycle wearing a crash helmet. This he quickly slipped off and, striding into the kitchen, set to work. An admiring crowd of cooks, stewards and small boys always collected to watch him. By the time he had finished, Sarah's cake looked as though it had been made at Claridges.

Then the presents began to pour in from Nigerian and European friends, including the Sultan, Sardauna, the ministers and other chiefs, whose generosity was most moving.

The Service was held at St Christopher's Church, a small brick building which could just hold two hundred people. The Bishop of Northern Nigeria conducted it, assisted by the army chaplain. Sarah wore a gown of white tulle and Nottingham lace, and a coronet of orange blossom which held her long veil in position. Our floral expert made her a professional looking bouquet of carnations picked in the garden that morning. Victor wore his white Colonial Service uniform and eight of his friends, in the same dress, provided a guard of honour. Sarah had two matrons of honour and one bridesmaid, Angela, all dressed in blue. Angela was accompanied by a page, the six-year-old son of the Chief Pilot of the Northern Communications flight. He, too, wore a miniature colonial service uniform complete with every detail from the white Wolsey helmet to the wellington boots and sword.

The ministers who were Christian and a small group of eminent Muslims attended the church service. The others, including the Sultan, the Emir of Zaria, the Premier and other Ministers joined the party for the reception. For many of them, it must have been the first Christian wedding they had ever attended.

The reception over, Sarah and Victor left in the Government House Rolls Royce which had so recently been 'royal', for a honeymoon at Tudun Wada.

Before we left Kaduna, we were to have two more royal visitors. The first of these was Princess Marina, then the Duchess of Kent. She called very briefly at Kano late at night on her way home after representing the Queen at the Ghana Independence Celebrations. The Ghanaians had greeted her politely but without marked enthusiasms, as Nkrumah was the man of the hour. She was therefore all the more surprised to find so many of the citizens of Kano lining the streets to wave and cheer. As she and Bryan drove past she even asked him why they were there.

The Emir had invited her to his palace to meet his council. He also conducted her on a tour of the house, the courtyards of which were lined with mounted retainers in full durbar regalia. He was accompanied by his little grandson, a toddler in an ankle-length gown. Princess Marina took the child by the hand and every now and then she bent down to talk to him. 'You know, you really ought to be in bed!' she said, with a smile.

Not long after this we were told that Her Majesty, Queen Elizabeth the Queen Mother would also be stopping for a short time at Kano. She was on her way back to London from Rhodesia. We took the train up to Kano and were at the airport early the next morning awaiting the arrival of her Britannia. It cruised in punctually at 6.40 a.m. The gangway was wheeled up. The door of the aircraft opened and there stood the Queen Mother, radiant and elegant in a white, lace dress and ostrich feathers hat, smiling at us. With Sardauna and the Resident of Kano, we walked forward to greet her. Bryan then took her slowly through the city to the Emir's Palace, through the streets which were, once again, crowded with cheering people. As the Queen Mother waved and smiled, the ostrich feathers on her hat billowed gracefully in the morning breeze.

It so happened the Emir of Kano was away in London at the time, undergoing an operation on his eyes for cataract. But he had arranged that the Queen Mother should meet his wives just as the Queen had done nine months earlier. Unfortunately, something went wrong with the timing arrangements in the inner recesses of the palace for when we reached the room where the meeting was to take place, we found it empty. 'Well, and where are they?' Her Majesty asked me. Of course, I hadn't the slightest idea. I went to the door of the room and looked desperately into the courtyard for someone to help. I spotted Angela, who had been tagging along at the rear of the procession with instructions to make herself inconspicuous. I told her what had happened and ended, 'Find Daddy and tell him to do something, quickly!' Angela disappeared and meanwhile I tried to engage the Queen Mother in conversation. Presently Angela reappeared, made her curtsey and said that the wives were just coming. Much to my relief, two minutes later in hurried two young women. They hoped the Queen Mother had arrived safely. They trusted that she had left the Queen in good health. They were so pleased to see her, oh so very pleased. In fact, they said all the right things several times over and meant them and we hoped Her Majesty forgave them for being so late.

When the Royal party arrived back at the airport and all the official Goodbyes had been said, the Lady in Waiting came to me and said, 'Queen Elizabeth wishes to say 'Goodbye' to Angela.' So a delighted little girl was produced from behind the VIP's to make her curtsey once more and to shake hands with our Royal guest.

We were by this time approaching the end of our time in Nigeria. Already two of the great chiefs and one other prominent Northerner had sought private interviews with me asking me to persuade Bryan to stay on. 'This self-government,' one of them said, 'What does it mean? We do not want it.' Another pleaded with me, 'You must tell your husband to stay with us. He will listen to you. We do not know what will happen if he goes.' I replied that he had made up his mind that this was the right time to go and that nothing I said was likely to have much effect. However, I would certainly pass on to him what they had said.

The ministers, however, did not plead for Bryan to stay. He felt that his duty lay to all classes and all peoples and he had exercised his powers as Governor to the end. There had, therefore, been inevitable differences of opinion between himself and the ministers. Yet, however much they sometimes disagreed with him, they knew that Bryan was doing his best for the North and they bore him no grudge.

The time was now close for our final 'Goodbye.' We began by farewell tours to the provisional centres. Then came the parties and receptions in Kaduna and the speech making. It was the familiar ritual of a Governor's farewell. Yet, to the North, Bryan was more than a Governor: he was their old friend, '*Mai Wandon Karfe*', who had lived and worked with them for thirty-seven years and had known most of their chiefs and ministers since their school days.

As we drove out of Government House and waved 'Goodbye' to our servants, Joseph, the Alis great and small, Audu, Nda and the rest, a lump rose obstinately in my throat and I fought with it all the way to the station where hundreds of people had gathered to say 'Goodbye'. At last, the soldiers played the Hausa Farewell, the train gathered steam and we moved slowly away.

INDEX

148

Gardens, 38
Girls' Training Centre, 68, 75, 85, 139
Great Salla of, 41–3
native administration (NA) in, 39–40
and see Sardauna of Sokoto, Sultan of
Sokoto
Sultan of Sokoto, 39, 41, 43, 109, 145,
knighted,139
South Africa, 58–9, 63

Tani, 75
Tanko, 11, 13, 15, 16, 18, 27, 30
Tchad, 11, 13, 15, 16, 18, 27, 30
Thompstone, Sir Eric, 99–100
Toby (terrier), 16
Tsetse belt, 7
Tuaregs, 34, 53
Tudan Wada, 129, 130, 134, 142
turmis, 20

Umaru, Dabai, 18, 19, 22–3
United African Company, 24, 115

United Middle Belt Congress (UMBC),
131–2
Usuman, 11–12, 13, 15, 16, 18, 21, 22,
23, 27, 30, 33, 34, 53
Usuman dan Fodio, 14, 40
Vichy French (France), 35–6, 44, 48
and see Guilbaud, Colonel,
Vigo, Mr. 82

Weatherhead, Sylvia, 100
Weatherhead, 'Waddle', 100
Williams, Conrad, 37–8, 40
Wilson. Mrs 'Rocks', 53–4
Women's Corona Society, 125
Wurin Idi, 42

Yauri, Emir of, 111

Zaria, 74, 121, 122
Zaria, Emir of, 145
Zinder, 36
Zungeru, 9, 16

ACKNOWLEDGEMENTS

My thanks are due to Mr A.H.M. Kirk-Greene for his ceaseless encouragement, also to Dr Helen Callaway for her valuable comments and advice. I am greatly indebted to Maurice Lately for his preface and to my sister, Barbara Lately, for her help in presentation and in many other ways. I thank Richard Barlow-Poole for his efforts on my behalf. I am also grateful to Reba Hind-Smith for typing the original manuscript and to Joan Brise for deciphering the second amended version some thirty years later. I also thank my family for their unfailing support.

Finally, I must pay tribute to my publisher, Dr Lester Crook, for his patience and perception.

Joan Sharwood-Smith   March 1990

To M.W.K. with love